Ready Readers:
Children's Literature
Volume I

CENTER FOR LIT

Design and layout by Emily Andrews
Copy editing by Megan Andrews and Ian Andrews

Cover art by J. Renee Illustration
www.jreneeillustration.com

OUR STORY

In 2003, Missy Andrews took a dare. A friend challenged her to show the parents in their homeschool co-op how to teach literature without a college degree, and she accepted. The method she devised became famous as *Teaching the Classics*, the teacher-training seminar that now equips parents and teachers all over the world to pass on the art of reading to their students.

Missy and her husband Adam founded CenterForLit shortly thereafter and began sharing the simple principles of *Teaching the Classics* with parents and teachers at conventions and speaking engagements nationwide. CenterForLit now offers curriculum materials, online classes, live teacher-training, and parent-teacher support networks, all dedicated to helping readers understand and revel in the beauty of classic books.

The world's great literature contains the wisdom of the ages – a treasure worth seeking. To readers who lack the proper tools, however, that treasure often remains locked away and hidden from sight.

Our mission is to supply you, the treasure seeker, with the right maps and keys.

TABLE OF CONTENTS

INTRODUCTION

The *Ready Readers* series is intended to assist the teacher or parent in conducting meaningful discussions of literature in the classroom or home school. It is important to note that *Ready Readers* are <u>not</u> intended to be workbooks for the student, but rather a model and guide for discussion leaders. Questions and answers follow the pattern presented in *Teaching the Classics*, CenterForLit's flagship literature seminar. Though the concepts underlying this approach to literary analysis are explained in detail in that seminar, the following brief summary presents the basic principles upon which this guide is based.

The *Teaching the Classics* approach to literary analysis and interpretation is built around **three unique ideas** which, when combined, produce a powerful instrument for understanding and teaching literature:

First: All works of fiction share the same basic elements — <u>Context, Structure, and Style</u>. A literature lesson that helps the student identify these elements in a story prepares him for meaningful discussion of the story's themes.

> <u>Context</u> encompasses all of the details of time and place surrounding the writing of a story, including the personal life of the author as well as historical events that shaped the author's world.

> <u>Structure</u> includes the essential building blocks that make up a story, and that all stories have in common: Conflict, Plot (which includes *exposition*, *rising action*, *climax*, *denouement*, and *conclusion*), Setting, Characters, and Theme.

> <u>Style</u> refers to the literary devices used by authors to create the mood and atmosphere of their stories. Recognition of some basic literary devices (alliteration, simile, personification, metaphor, etc.) enables a reader not only to understand the author's themes more readily, but also to appreciate his craftsmanship more fully.

Second: Because it is approachable and engaging, <u>children's literature</u> is the best genre to employ in teaching the foundational principles of literary analysis. Children's books present these building blocks in clear, memorable language, and are thus treasure mines of opportunities for the astute teacher — allowing him to present Context, Structure, and Style with ease to children and adults alike. Having learned to recognize these basic elements in the simple text of a classic children's story, a student is well prepared to analyze complex works suitable for his own age and level of intellectual development.

Third: The best classroom technique for teaching literary analysis and interpretation is the <u>Socratic Method</u>. Named after the ancient gadfly who first popularized this style of teaching, the Socratic method employs the art of questioning, rather than lecturing, to accomplish education. Based upon the conviction that the process of discovery constitutes the better part of learning, our program uses well-placed questions to teach students *how* to think, rather than dictating to them *what* to think.

The *Teaching the Classics* seminar syllabus supplies a thorough list of Socratic questions for teachers to use in class discussion. The questions are general enough to be used with any book, but focused enough to lead the student into meaningful contemplation of the themes of even the most difficult stories. Questions on the list are arranged in order of difficulty: from grammar-level questions which ask for the mere fact of a story, to rhetoric-level questions which require discussion of ideologies and transcendent themes. Properly employed, this list can help teachers engage their classes in important discussions of ideas, and can also provide a rich resource for essay and other writing assignments! Used in conjunction with a good writing program, *Teaching the Classics* produces **deep thinkers** at any age.

The questions used in this guide have been taken directly from the Socratic list, and will therefore be familiar to the seminar alumnus.

More information about *Teaching the Classics* may be found at www.centerforlit.com.

Happy reading!

Adam Andrews, Director
The Center for Literary Education
3350 Beck Road
Rice, WA 99167
(509) 738-6837
adam@centerforlit.com

A NOTE ON THIS EDITION

Ready Readers: Children's Literature, Vol. 1 is a reprinting of our original publication *Ready Readers: 10 Lessons in Comprehension and Analysis* with minor edits and additions.

The *Children's Literature* series is intended to assist teachers and parents with students **of all ages**. With the simpler Socratic questions, a discussion of a good picture book can familiarize students **at or below** this reading level with the basic elements of a story and the experience of discussion, building a foundation for upper level literary analysis.

For students **above** this reading level, picture books provide an easy entry into the *Teaching the Classics* method for literary discussion. The stories covered in this volume share the same story elements as Tolstoy's *War and Peace.* However, the brevity and simplicity of the picture books will allow the student quick access to the parts of story needed for literary analysis. In fact at CenterForLit, we suggest that all students K-12 begin the year by discussing a picture book in order to reacquaint themselves with the method before continuing on to literature at their own reading level.

References: The numbers in parentheses following each Socratic question refer to the complete Socratic List, which is included in the back of the course syllabus for CenterForLit's flagship seminar, *Teaching the Classics: A Socratic Method for Literary Education.*

ABOUT THE AUTHOR

Missy Andrews is co-founder of CenterForLit and a homeschooling mother of six. She graduated summa cum laude from Hillsdale College in 1991 with a BA in English Literature and Christian Studies. Missy and her husband Adam teach in their local homeschool co-op and conduct online literature classes for students around the world. She is currently pursuing her Master of Arts degree in Imaginative Literature.

Mem Fox's
Harriet, You'll Drive Me Wild!

Questions for Socratic Discussion
by Missy Andrews

CENTER FOR LIT

TABLE OF CONTENTS:
HARRIET, YOU'LL DRIVE ME WILD!

QUICK CARD

Reference	*Harriet, You'll Drive Me Wild!* by Mem Fox ISBN-10: 0152045988 ISBN-13: 978-0152045982
Plot	When Harriet's antics cause her frazzled mother to lose her temper in spite of her attempts at self-control, the two learn to forgive one another.
Setting	• Harriet's pre-school years • A family home • An average day
Characters	Harriet, a young girl Harriet's mother (protagonist)
Conflict	Man vs. Man: Harriet's childish mistakes make life difficult for her mother. Man vs. Self: Harriet's mother struggles to keep her temper.
Theme	Harriet and her mother build relationship through repentance and forgiveness. Universal Issues Include: • Self-Control • Patience • Motherly love • Childishness
Literary Devices	• Repetition • Rhyme • Alliteration

QUESTIONS ABOUT STRUCTURE: SETTING

What is the mood or atmosphere of the place where the story happens? Is it cheerful and sunny, or dark and bleak? (1d)

The story takes place in a home. The mood of the story is warm and lighthearted.

Among what kinds of people is the story set? (1h)

The characters are ordinary people – a mother and her little girl. They seem a typical, middle class family.

On what day does the story happen? What time of day? (2a)

The story transpires over the course of a single day.

In what time of life for the main characters do the events occur? Are they children? Are they just passing into adulthood? Are they already grownups? (2e)

The story transpires over the course of a single day. It happens in Harriet's childhood and the mother's early parenting years. Harriet has the energy of an average 2-4-year-old. She is into everything, a very busy child.

NOTES:

_____

_____

_____

_____

_____

_____

QUESTIONS ABOUT STRUCTURE: CHARACTERS

Who is the story about? (3)

> The main character is Harriet's mother. She is harried because her young daughter is so very busy. She, like many mothers, wants to gently correct her daughter, who exasperates her with foolish behavior at every turn.

Is the character kind, gentle, stern, emotional, harsh, logical, rational, compassionate or exacting…? Make up a list of adjectives that describe the protagonist. (3f)

> The mother is patient, understanding, calm, gentle, exhausted, exasperated, sinful, angry, sorry, repentant, and good-natured at various points in the story's development.

What does the character do for a living? Is he a professional, or a blue-collar worker? (3h)

> Although this detail is not explicitly mentioned, the context of the story leads readers to believe the mother is a stay-at-home mom.

What do other characters think or say about the protagonist? (3k)

> The narrator repeatedly says that Harriet's mother "didn't like to yell." Instead she would sigh when Harriet's behavior caused mayhem and say, "Harriet, you foolish child, Harriet, you'll drive me wild."

What does the protagonist think is the most important thing in life? How do you know this? Does the protagonist say this out loud, or do his thoughts and actions give him away? (3m)

> Clearly, the mother thinks it important to raise her child with forbearance and patience. Both her words and actions communicate this. She thinks loving Harriet is most important. However, her second motivation is accomplishing the work of housekeeping, and it is the war between these two desires that creates the majority of the story's conflict.

Do the protagonist's priorities change over the course of the story? In what way? What causes this change? Is it a change for the better, or for the worse? (3n)

> Although the mother's priorities never change, her ability to achieve them is challenged as the story progresses. "And then Harriet's mother began to yell…" Certainly this loss of self-control is no merit, except that it gives the mother the chance to repent to her child and communicate love to her in the process. The disaster, in this way, becomes a means to closer relationship with her child.

Is the protagonist a type or archetype? Is he an "Everyman" with whom the reader is meant to identify? Are his struggles symbolic of human life generally in some way? (3p)

Harriet's mother is, indeed, an archetypical mother, beset with the familiar struggles and challenges all moms face and motivated by the same maternal love and compassion. Most mothers would identify with her.

Is the protagonist a sympathetic character? Do you identify with him and hope he will succeed? Do you pity him? Do you scorn or despise his weakness in some way? Why? (3q)

Since she is easy to understand, she is a sympathetic character. What mother doesn't sigh to find her child has created a new mess for her to clean up? What mother doesn't at some point lose her cool when her child's foolish behavior interrupts her adult priorities one time too many? All she wants to do is get one thing done and keep it so! Poor mommy!

Who else is the story about? (4)

Harriet, the child, is curious and careless. She is not overtly rebellious, just active and heedless. She hasn't yet learned to foresee disaster and avoid it. In short, she is a child! Yet she is an antagonist by definition because she throws up obstacles that keep the mother from her goals.

In what way is he antagonistic? What goal of the protagonist is he opposed to? (4b)

It's not so much that Harriet is even aware of the obstacles she poses. The trials she creates for her mother are not intentional. She is a toddler and a mess-maker. When she sees the trouble she has caused, she is truly sorry.

Does the author believe this character to be responsible for his own sinfulness, or does he believe him a product of a "negative environment"? (4l) Is the antagonist truly evil, by definition, or is he merely antagonistic to the protagonist by virtue of his vocation or duty? (4m)

The child is not condemned for her foolishness. She is not evil. She is merely immature, lacking the foresight necessary to avoid the accidents she causes.

What are the antagonist's surroundings? Are they related to his character? Did the author put him there on purpose? (4n)

A mess follows Harriet wherever she goes. (Dripping paint, spilled food, flying feathers from ripped pillows.)

NOTES:

_____

_____

_____

_____

_____

_____

_____

_____

_____

_____

_____

_____

_____

_____

_____

_____

_____

_____

_____

QUESTIONS ABOUT STRUCTURE: CONFLICT AND PLOT

What does the mother want? (5)

Mom wants several things, including:

- A moment's peace

- To accomplish something

- Harriet to stop acting foolishly

- Patience and self-control.

Does he attempt to overcome something – a physical impediment, or an emotional handicap? (5b)

To accomplish these things, she must gently admonish Harriet for her behavior and patiently teach her to think ahead. She must exercise self-denial and self-control, placing the needs of her daughter ahead of her own needs.

Is the conflict an external one, having to do with circumstances in the protagonist's physical world, or is it an internal conflict, taking place in his mind and emotions? (5e)

The conflict is both external and internal. Externally, she must continually clean up messy Harriet's mistakes, admonishing her to think ahead. Internally, she must remain unimpassioned and patient.

Why can't the protagonist have what she wants? (6)

The main obstacle mother faces is her own limitations: her temper. She does not have endless patience. Her outburst, however justified, is as wrong as the actions of young Harriet which provoke it.

What kind of conflict is represented in the story? (6g-k)

This is a man vs. man and a man vs. self conflict since she struggles both with Harriet and with her own temper.

What happens in the story? (8) What major events take place in the story as a result of the conflict? (8a)

> Harriet is a messy child. She spills her milk and food when she accidentally pulls the tablecloth off the table at dinner. She damages the rug when she brings her still-wet painting through the house to show her mother, dripping paint along the way. Finally, Harriet's mother loses her patience when, during naptime, Harriet's tousle with her dog results in a ripped pillow and a room full of feathers. Despite her efforts at self-control, Harriet's mother gets angry and yells at her daughter.

How is the main problem solved? (9) Does the protagonist get what he's after? (9a)

> The story's climax occurs when a "terrible silence" is followed by the mother's yell. Once her anger is spent, she sees her own foolishness and apologizes to her daughter. When all is forgiven, the two clean up the "big mess," laughing together.

Is the situation pleasantly resolved, or is it resolved in a terrible way? (9c)

> The mother's outburst is a terrible event, one that she'd worked hard to avoid.

What events form the highest point or climax of the story's tension? Are they circumstantial events, or emotional ones? Is the climax a spiritual or physical one? (9d)

> This is a tense, emotional climax. The mother's nerves are stretched too thin. Her human sinfulness gets in the way of her better self.

After the climax of the story, did you wonder how it would end? How does it end? How are the "loose ends" tied up? Were all of your questions answered? (10a)

> The story resolves pleasantly since the mother's love for Harriet leads her to take responsibility for her outburst and repent. Harriet and her mother, both prone to mistakes, find fellowship in their inadvertent failures and foolishness. As a result, their relationship is strengthened.

Do you believe the characters' responses to the cataclysmic events, or are they anti-climactic in some regard? (10c)

> Because of this, it's perhaps better that the outburst occurred than if it had not. Now, Harriet and her mother understand one another in a better way, and know one another's love in forgiveness.

QUESTIONS ABOUT STRUCTURE: THEME

What does the protagonist learn? (11)

The protagonist learns that she herself needs grace, forgiveness, and patience for her shortfalls as much as does her little Harriet.

Are other people in the story ennobled, changed, saved, improved or otherwise affected by the story's events? (12a)

The two characters laugh at themselves together at the story's end. The tension is diffused in self-awareness and covered by love.

Do they re-examine their values and ideas? (12e)

The mother doesn't so much reevaluate her values, but affirms them in the end by her response to her own failure. She is committed to loving Harriet in spite of herself.

What is the main idea of the story? (13)

This story deals with the universal problem of sin. While Harriet's mother wants to control her temper and deal gently with her daughter, her own impatience and frustration make this a difficult matter.

Does the story offer an answer to a particular problem associated with one of those themes? (13b)

The story seems to offer repentance, reconciliation, and forgiveness as solutions to the problem of sin.

What answer does the story seem to suggest for the question, "What is a good life?" (13d)

The story seems to suggest that a good life is a life of self-control, patience, repentance, and forgiveness, all of which contribute to relationships and peace.

NOTES:

_____

_____

_____

QUESTIONS ABOUT STYLE

Does the author use the sounds of our language to create interest in her story? (14)

- **Rhyme**

"Harriet, you foolish child, Harriet, you'll drive me wild."

"…what are we to do?...I'm talking to you."

"…instead she said…"

- **Repetition**

"just like that…"

"…and she was."

- **Alliteration**

"feathers flew"

"Harriet Harris"

"…she dribbled jam on her jeans…"

"…Harriet was painting a picture; she dripped paint onto the carpet…"

NOTES:

_____

_____

_____

_____

QUESTIONS ABOUT CONTEXT

Who is the author? (18)

Australian-born Mem Fox has written 25 noted children's books. Among these are the heartwarming *Wilfrid Gordon McDonald Partridge* and the swashbuckling *Tough Boris*. In addition to children's literature, Ms. Fox has authored *Reading Magic*, a book aimed at parents of pre-school children, and *Radical Reflections: Passionate Opinions on Teaching, Learning and Living*, a teacher's text. In addition to her zeal for teaching, she is actively involved in a literacy campaign, writing what she terms the "literature of liberation…from the tyranny of the attitudes and expectations that the world thrusts upon each of us."

As a child, Ms. Fox lived in Zimbabwe where her parents worked as missionaries for Hope Fountain. As a young adult she attended drama school in England, where she met her future husband. She married Malcolm Fox in 1969, and has one daughter, Chloe, now a journalist and high school teacher. She served as Assistant Professor at Flinders University in Adelaide, Australia, for 24 years, a position from which she has since retired. Currently, she maintains a full schedule writing and traveling abroad both to promote her books and to champion literacy.

NOTES:

_____

_____

_____

_____

_____

_____

_____

_____

STORY CHARTS

The following pages contain story charts of the type presented in the live seminar *Teaching the Classics.* As is made clear in that seminar, a separate story chart may be constructed for each of the conflicts present in a work of fiction. In particular, the reader's decision as to the ***climax*** and central ***themes*** of the plot structure will depend upon his understanding of the story's central ***conflict***. As a result, though the details of setting, characters, exposition, and conclusion may be identical from analysis to analysis, significant variation may be found in those components which appear down the center of the story chart: Conflict, Climax, and Theme. This of course results from the fact that literary interpretation is the work of active minds, and differences of opinion are to be expected – even encouraged!

For the teacher's information, one story chart has been filled in on the next page. In addition, a blank chart is included to allow the teacher to examine different conflicts in the same format.

Harriet, You'll Drive Me Wild! by Mem Fox: Story Chart

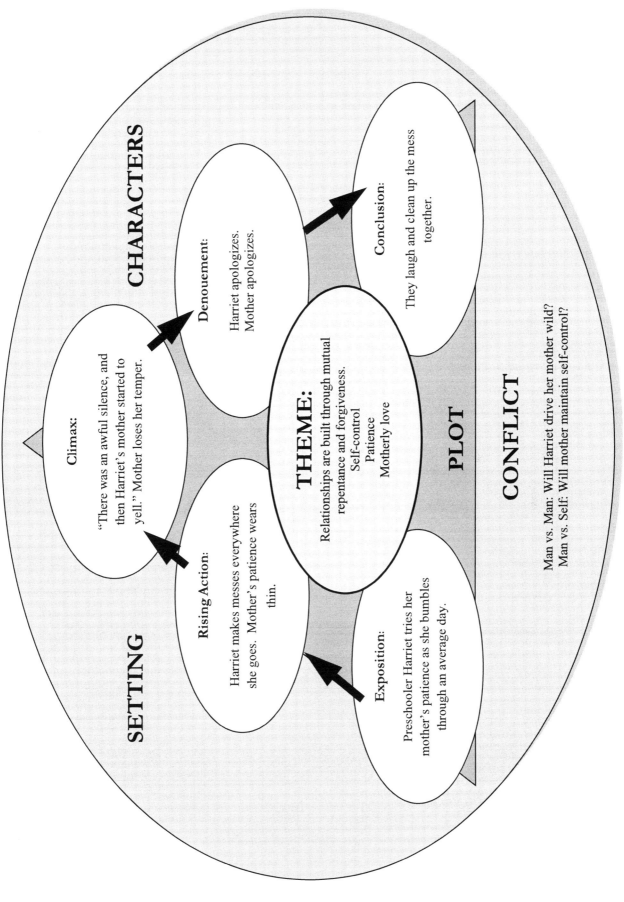

CHARACTERS

SETTING

Climax:
"There was an awful silence, and then Harriet's mother started to yell." Mother loses her temper.

Denouement:
Harriet apologizes.
Mother apologizes.

Conclusion:
They laugh and clean up the mess together.

Rising Action:
Harriet makes messes everywhere she goes. Mother's patience wears thin.

THEME:
Relationships are built through mutual repentance and forgiveness.
Self-control
Patience
Motherly love

Exposition:
Preschooler Harriet tries her mother's patience as she bumbles through an average day.

PLOT

CONFLICT

Man vs. Man: Will Harriet drive her mother wild?
Man vs. Self: Will mother maintain self-control?

Harriet, You'll Drive Me Wild! by Mem Fox: Blank Story Chart

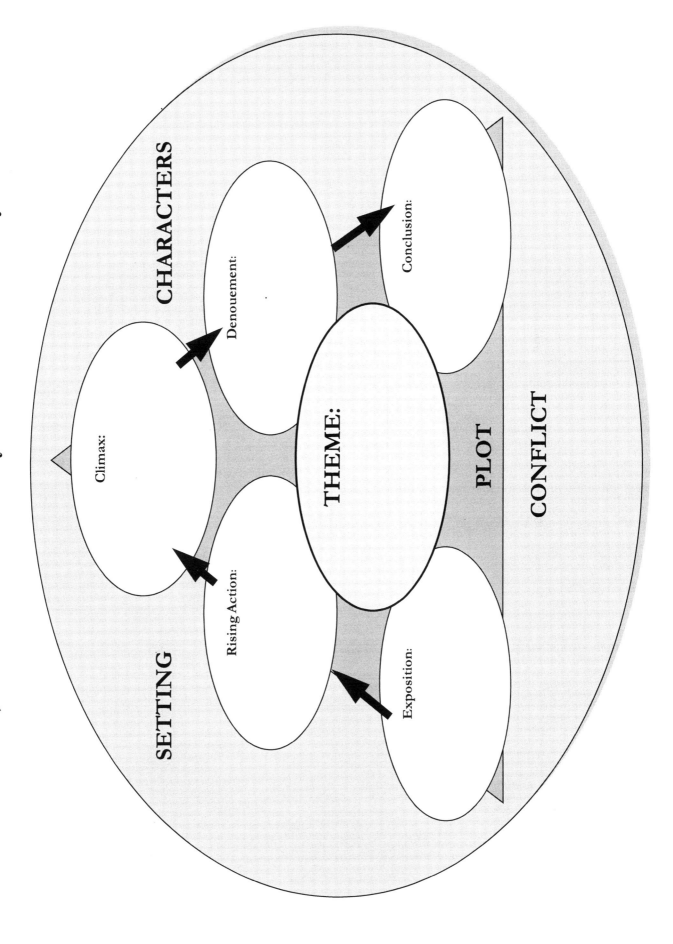

CHARACTERS

SETTING

THEME:

PLOT

CONFLICT

Climax:

Denouement:

Conclusion:

Rising Action:

Exposition:

Evaline Ness's
Sam, Bangs & Moonshine

Questions for Socratic Discussion
by Missy Andrews

CENTER FOR LIT

TABLE OF CONTENTS:
SAM, BANGS & MOONSHINE

QUICK CARD

Reference	*Sam, Bangs & Moonshine* by Evaline Ness ISBN-10: 0805003150 ISBN-13: 978-0805003154
Plot	Young, motherless Samantha is left alone daily with only her wild imagination and her pet cat, Bangs, to entertain her. Her neighbor friend, Thomas, relishes and believes her fantastic stories. Her fisherman father encourages her to forsake such "moonshine" for reality and truthfulness. Still, Sam persists in telling whoppers. When her falsehoods nearly cost Thomas and Bangs their lives, she learns a mighty lesson.
Setting	A small island near a large harbor. A fishing village.
Characters	Samantha – the daughter of a New England fisherman, this motherless child invents wild stories to comfort and entertain herself in her father's absence. Samantha's father – a New England fisherman whose wife's death has left him solely responsible for rearing his small, imaginative daughter. His gentle yet stern manner leads his daughter to thoughtfully contemplate her lying and its gravity. Bangs – Sam's loyal and wise cat Thomas – Sam's faithful, believing friend
Conflict	Man vs. Nature Man vs. Himself
Theme	– Lies are dangerous and harmful to you and others. The truth, however plain or painful, is always better. – Lying vs. Imagination – Moonshine/ Flummadiddle
Literary Devices	Imagery Irony

QUESTIONS ABOUT STRUCTURE: SETTING

In what country or region does the story happen? (1a) Does the story happen in one spot, or does the action unfold across a wide area? (1c)

The story takes place on an island near a large harbor in a fishing village.

What is the mood or atmosphere of the place where the story happens? Is it cheerful and sunny, or dark and bleak? (1d)

The atmosphere, influenced by the unpredictable and somewhat violent weather patterns, is foreboding and brooding.

Is the setting a real or imaginary place? If it's imaginary, is it subject to the same physical laws as our world is? (1g)

Although the author never names her town, countless towns like it exist both in New England and Canada.

Among what kinds of people is the story set? What is their economic class? How do they live? Are they hopeful? Downtrodden? Depressed? Why? (1h)

The people in this town work hard for their living. These old salts are realists, who pit their strength and wit against nature regularly. They haven't the luxury of vain imaginations since their livelihood depends upon overcoming the realities that nature deals them.

When does the story happen? (2) How long a period of time does the story cover? A few minutes? A single day? A whole lifetime? (2b)

The story covers a single day in Sam's life.

In what time of life for the main characters do the events occur? Are they children? Are they just passing into adulthood? Are they already grownups? Does setting the story in this particular time of the characters' lives make the story better? (2e)

In particular, the story takes place in Sam's childhood. This is significant, since Sam's fertile and unrestrained imagination is indicative of childhood.

NOTES:

_____

_____

_____

_____

_____

_____

_____

_____

_____

_____

_____

_____

_____

_____

_____

_____

_____

_____

QUESTIONS ABOUT STRUCTURE: CHARACTERS

Who is the story about? (3)

The protagonist is Sam, the daughter of a New England fisherman. A motherless child, she invents wild stories to comfort and entertain herself in her father's absence.

What does the protagonist look like (hair, eyes, height, build, etc.)? (3d)

She is small, perhaps 7 or 8 years old. She carries more responsibility than most her age.

Is the character kind, gentle, stern, emotional, harsh, logical, rational, compassionate or exacting…? Make up a list of adjectives that describe the protagonist. What words or actions on the protagonist's part make you choose the adjectives you do? (3f)

Sam is: imaginative, sad, creative, heedless, isolated, lonely, fanciful, self-absorbed, and shortsighted at various points in the story.

What does the character say about herself to other people? (3j)

Sam says she is "special." She claims to have a mermaid mother. She fancies herself a magic carpet rider and believes her pet cat, Bangs, can talk.

What do other characters think or say about her? (3k)

Thomas, her wealthy and naïve neighbor friend, thinks she's all she claims to be. He believes her utterly. Her father says she's full of moonshine and flumadiddle.

Is the character a member of any particular religious or social group? If so, what do you know about this group? What motivates this group? What do its members feel to be important? (3l)

Since her father's livelihood and safety depend on clear thinking (i.e. realism), truth is most important to her father.

What does the protagonist think is the most important thing in life? How do you know this? Does the protagonist say this out loud, or do his thoughts and actions give him away? (3m)

Sam considers her imagination, her dad, and her pet cat, Bangs, most important.

Do the protagonist's priorities change over the course of the story? In what way? What causes this change? Is it a change for the better, or for the worse? (3n)

> Over the course of the story, Sam's priorities change. People become more important than her daydreams. Since their well-being depends upon her truthfulness, the truth becomes more valuable to Sam, as well.

Is the protagonist a sympathetic character? Do you identify with him and hope he will succeed? Do you pity him? Do you scorn or despise his weakness in some way? Why? (3q)

> The child is a sympathetic character. Readers pity her loneliness and understand her need to create a fantasy world.

Who else is the story about? (4)

> Thomas – Sam's wealthy and naïve neighbor friend. Younger than Sam, he believes everything Sam says and idolizes her.

> Bangs – Sam's pet cat. Sam is sure he speaks to her, sometimes comforting, sometimes upbraiding, but always loving. Bangs acts like Sam's conscience.

> Father – A New England fisherman and a single father, he is both gentle and stern. He wants Sam to speak sense instead of moonshine. Capable and strong, he saves Thomas.

> **NOTES:**
>
> _____
>
> _____
>
> _____
>
> _____
>
> _____
>
> _____
>
> _____

QUESTIONS ABOUT STRUCTURE: CONFLICT AND PLOT

What does the main character want? (5)

Sam wants:

-To entertain and amuse herself in her loneliness

-To "be" someone special

-To rise above and beyond her condition and circumstances

-To escape reality

-To achieve freedom, peace, contentment, relationship

Why can't she have it? (6)

In her attempts to escape her loneliness, Sam fails to appreciate the good in her life. She pities herself. (Man vs. Self)

No one can escape reality. Despite her attempts to live in a fairytale, Sam cannot evade the real circumstances of her life or the real consequences of her actions. (Man vs. God or Fate)

She won't be honest with herself or others. Her lies lead Thomas into danger and produce the plot-driving action of the story. (Man vs. Self, Man vs. Man)

What other problems exist in the story? (7)

The conflict that propels the plot is Sam's lie to Thomas. She sends him out to a rock to find her "mermaid" mother just before high tide submerges it. Her cat stalks off after him. Both are endangered when a storm blows up. Will Sam's father reach them in time to save them? This crisis presents Man vs. Man and Man vs. Nature conflicts.

Are there other characters who don't understand the protagonist's motives and ambitions? (7d)

Sam's father struggles against her actions, although he tries to understand and must guess at her loneliness. Thomas probably can't understand her reticence to befriend him. He seems to live a "normal" life (i.e. two parents, a big house on the hill, a new bike). He probably can't fathom Sam's loss and loneliness. Even Sam herself may not understand why she does what she does. Most children aren't self-aware enough to consider their deeper intentions. They just act and react in response to their unnamed feelings.

Are there larger issues, (a larger context or frame) in which conflict exists and forms a background for the story (A war setting, for example)? (7f)

The conflict within Sam's heart (her dissatisfaction with reality) is the conflict beneath her lie to Thomas and his ensuing danger.

What happens in the story? (8)

Sam's lie sends Thomas into danger.

Sam ignores the implications of her lie at first, but when Bangs follows Thomas and the weather turns, she begins to fear.

Her father's disapproval intensifies her discomfort.

How is the problem solved? (9)

The circumstantial conflict is resolved when Sam's father rescues Thomas and Bangs turns up at Sam's window. The deeper conflict, Sam's reluctance to accept and live in reality, begins to be healed when she sees the danger of her "moonshine" and decides to live in truth. Her loneliness is addressed when she gives Thomas her new "baby kangaroo," an overture of friendship.

How does the story end? (10) Were you satisfied with the resolution? If not, why not? (10b)

It is hard to be entirely satisfied with the story's resolution. It is good that Sam has learned to tell the truth. However, her forced entry into reality provides no real happy ending. She will continue to be alone much of the time. She will continue motherless. She will probably still want much. She has learned to embrace the real, but her reality is somewhat wanting.

NOTES:

_____

_____

_____

_____

_____

QUESTIONS ABOUT STRUCTURE: THEME

Does the main character explain to the reader his perspective on the events that have transpired? (11e)

Sam's heart is changed when her lies threaten to take the only real relationships she has. Moonshine is flumadiddle. Real is Bangs and Father and Thomas.

Is he sacrificed in some way? (was this a part of the climax or resolution?) (11d)

In a sense, Sam's childhood is abandoned when she forsakes moonshine for reality.

What do the other characters learn? (12)

No other characters are changed. In particular, her father remains unchanged. It would perhaps have been more satisfying if he had seen and met his daughter's need in some way.

What is the main idea of the story? (13)

Sam, the young daughter of a New England fisherman, spends her days in lonely solitude. Since the death of her mother, she keeps house for her father and entertains herself during his long absences with wild imaginings and heart-to-heart conversations with her beloved cat, Bangs. Occasionally, she is visited by Thomas, the little neighbor boy who lives in the large house on the hill. Younger than Sam, Thomas naively believes every idle word Sam utters. Because she favors the landscape of her imagination over the sometimes bleaker substance of her life, Sam invents fantastical stories to tell Thomas.

On a particular day, one such story sends Thomas to a lonely strip of beach in search of Sam's "pet kangaroo" and "mermaid" mother. Bangs "speaks" to her, voicing the complaint of her conscience, and wanders off in Thomas's direction. When a fierce storm and an early tide trap Thomas on a rock, Sam's father goes to his aid. Alone, Sam waits anxiously for their return. However, even in the face of such possible catastrophe, Sam's heedless and selfish thoughts are filled only with concern for her cat. Although Thomas is retrieved, Bangs is declared lost. Faced with the painful consequences of her own lies, Sam is encouraged by her father to learn the difference between reality and moonshine.

While Sam's difficult circumstances create a man vs. nature conflict within the story, a larger struggle exists within Sam's heart, mind and conscience. Sam must decide if she will embrace real life, or live in a fiction. Her father, whom she trusts, and her conscience, which voices itself through her cat, nudge her towards reality. Yet, she resolutely resists this until her circumstances become more fearful than her fiction.

While retaining her vivid imagination, she gratefully acknowledges the friends, family, and favored pet that compose her real world, counting them more important than the loss her fictions mask.

This decision to embrace a real cup only half-full in lieu of a brimming cup of fantasy represents an intensely human dilemma. The ability to choose reality is a mark of maturity. Yet, the courage required to choose the real and forsake fancies often comes only when the "real" is threatened. In this manner, averted trauma replaces the heart's fear and misgivings with gratitude, the substance of acknowledged reality and the cornerstone of peace.

What answer does the story seem to suggest for the question, "What is a good life?" (13d)

According to this story, a good life is a life lived in reality.

NOTES:

_____

_____

_____

_____

_____

_____

_____

_____

_____

_____

_____

QUESTIONS ABOUT STYLE

Does the author use the characters and events in his story to communicate a theme that goes beyond them in some way? (17)

> **Irony:** One of the central themes of the story is to forsake "moonshine" and live in reality. This is ironic in light of the fact that the author was the wife of Eliot Ness, the famous Prohibition agent.

NOTES:

_____

_____

_____

_____

_____

_____

_____

_____

_____

_____

_____

QUESTIONS ABOUT CONTEXT

Who is the author? (18)

Evaline Michelow Ness was born April 24, 1911, in Union City, Ohio. Initially intending to become a fashion artist, she attended Ball State Teachers College (1931-32) and Chicago Art Institute (1933-35). Shortly thereafter, she married the renowned FBI agent, Elliot Ness. She obtained additional schooling at Corcoran Art School and at Academia di Belle Arte in Rome. In 1960, Mrs. Ness illustrated her first children's book, *The Bridge*, by Charles Osborn. Three years later, she wrote and illustrated *Josephina February*. However, it was her sensitively written portrayal of a lonely, imaginative girl in *Sam, Bangs, and Moonshine* which won her a Caldecott Medal in 1967. Two other books by Mrs. Ness, *Tom Tit Tot* ('66) and *A Pocketful of Cricket* ('65) also won the Caldecott Medal. Intent to create the appearance of texture on the printed page, Mrs. Ness used woodcutting, serigraphy, rubber-roller, ink splattering, and spitting techniques. Mrs. Ness died in New York in 1986.

NOTES:

_____

_____

_____

_____

_____

_____

_____

_____

STORY CHARTS

The following pages contain story charts of the type presented in the live seminar *Teaching the Classics.* As is made clear in that seminar, a separate story chart may be constructed for each of the conflicts present in a work of fiction. In particular, the reader's decision as to the **climax** and central **themes** of the plot structure will depend upon his understanding of the story's central **conflict**. As a result, though the details of setting, characters, exposition, and conclusion may be identical from analysis to analysis, significant variation may be found in those components which appear down the center of the story chart: Conflict, Climax, and Theme. This of course results from the fact that literary interpretation is the work of active minds, and differences of opinion are to be expected – even encouraged!

For the teacher's information, one story chart has been filled in on the next page. In addition, a blank chart is included to allow the teacher to examine different conflicts in the same format.

Sam, Bangs & Moonshine by Evaline Ness: Story Chart

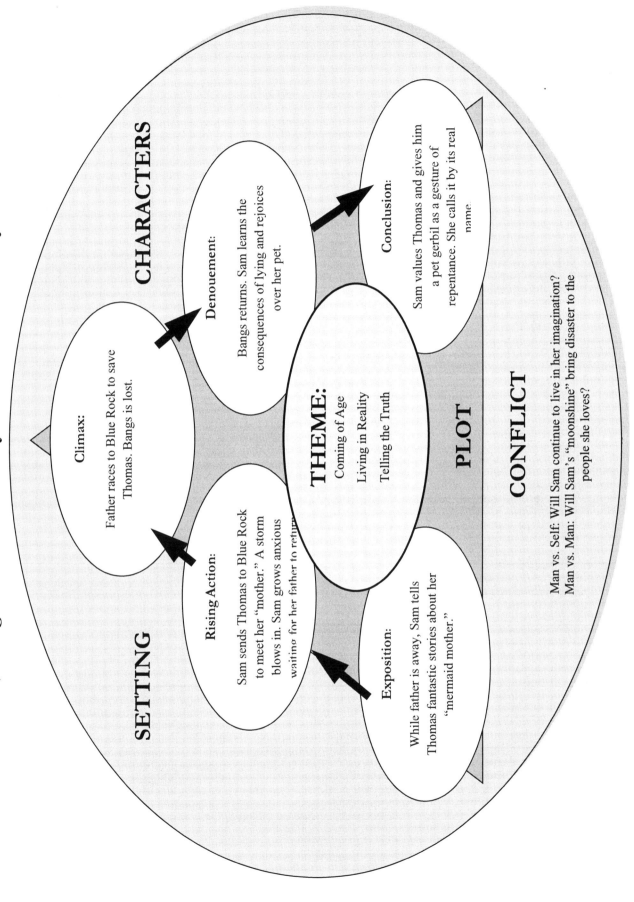

CHARACTERS

SETTING

Climax:
Father races to Blue Rock to save Thomas. Bangs is lost.

Denouement:
Bangs returns. Sam learns the consequences of lying and rejoices over her pet.

Conclusion:
Sam values Thomas and gives him a pet gerbil as a gesture of repentance. She calls it by its real name.

Rising Action:
Sam sends Thomas to Blue Rock to meet her "mother." A storm blows in. Sam grows anxious waiting for her father to return.

THEME:
Coming of Age
Living in Reality
Telling the Truth

PLOT

Exposition:
While father is away, Sam tells Thomas fantastic stories about her "mermaid mother."

CONFLICT

Man vs. Self: Will Sam continue to live in her imagination?
Man vs. Man: Will Sam's "moonshine" bring disaster to the people she loves?

Sam, Bangs & Moonshine by Evaline Ness: Blank Story Chart

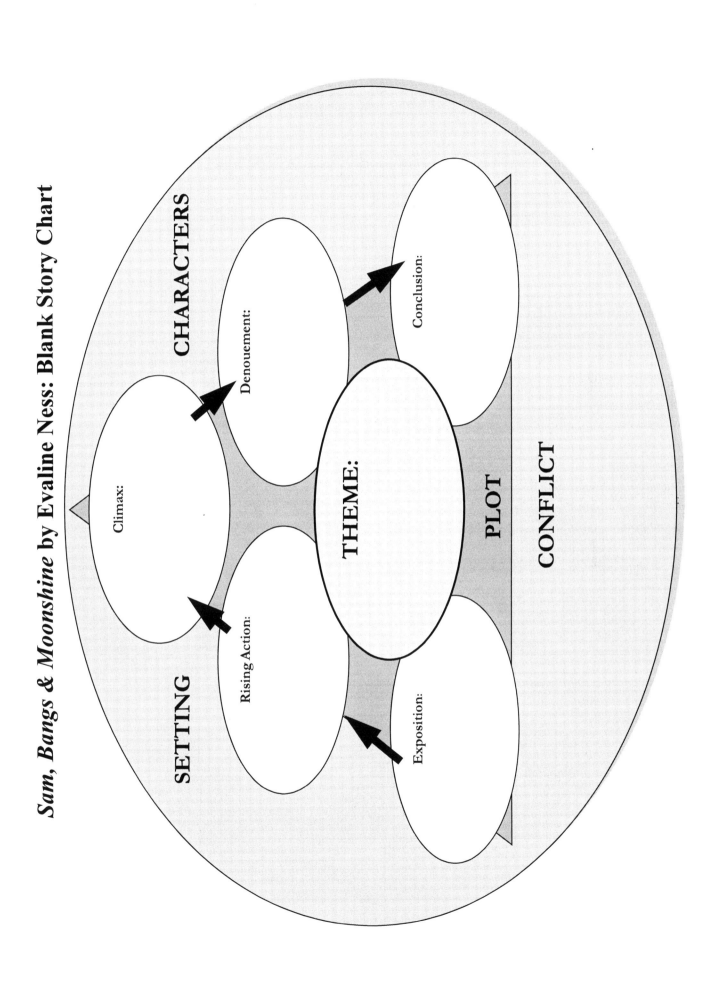

CHARACTERS

SETTING

CONFLICT

PLOT

THEME:

Climax:

Denouement:

Conclusion:

Rising Action:

Exposition:

Deborah Hopkinson's
Apples to Oregon

Questions for Socratic Discussion
by Missy Andrews

CENTER FOR LIT

TABLE OF CONTENTS:
APPLES TO OREGON

QUICK CARD

Reference	*Apples to Oregon* by Deborah Hopkinson ISBN-10: 0689847696 ISBN-13: 978-0689847696
Plot	Daddy and his daughter Delicious fight the forces of nature on the Oregon Trail to deliver their traveling nursery safely to a new home in Oregon.
Setting	The Oregon Trail in the 19th century. A wagon train headed west in the United States during the period of Western expansion.
Characters	Delicious (the narrator) Daddy Momma Delicious's brothers and sisters The Orchard Trees (Daddy's "babies")
Conflict	Delicious wants to help Daddy. Daddy and Delicious want to keep the plants alive on their journey to Oregon. (Man vs. Nature) Obstacles along the way include the Platte River (which represents the danger of drowning) and other forces of nature, including the windstorm, hail stones, drought, and frost.
Theme	Courage Diligence Cooperation Family relationships Fruits of labor Perseverance Determination Self-sacrifice Providence
Literary Devices	Alliteration Simile Personification Metaphor Allusion

QUESTIONS ABOUT STRUCTURE: SETTING

Where does the story take place? (1) In what country or region does the story happen? (1a) Does the story happen in one spot, or does the action unfold across a wide area? (1c)

The story takes place on America's Oregon Trail during the period of Western expansion, and that's "no place for babies!" Consequently, the action unfolds across a vast area beginning in the interior U.S. and ending on the West coast in the Oregon territory.

The setting of this story proves crucial both to character development and plot, since the characters' natural surroundings present the main obstacles to their goals.

Among what kinds of people is the story set? What is their economic class? How do they live? Are they hopeful? Downtrodden? Depressed? Why? (1h)

The people that made this trek were a hearty, industrious and resourceful set. They endured great hardships and deprivations in order to people the uninhabited wilds.

When does the story happen? (2)

The real trip upon which Mrs. Hopkinson's story is based occurred in 1847 when Henderson Luelling left his home in Salem, Iowa to establish a fruit orchard six miles south of Portland in Milwaukie, Oregon.

In what season does the story take place? (2c)

The action begins when the wagon train sets out in spring, as soon as roads are passable, and continues through the fall when frost threatens to undo all their efforts.

In what time of life for the main characters do the events occur? Are they children? Are they just passing into adulthood? Are they already grownups? Does setting the story in this particular time of the characters' lives make the story better? (2e)

In addition to the historic setting, the story occurs in the childhood of the narrator, Delicious. In the eyes of this young girl, her pioneer daddy is a hero whose genius and work ethic will make him famous with his family and history. Her childlike faith in her father mitigates not only the obstacles of nature, but also the discouraging words of naysayers along the trail.

In what intellectual period is the story set? What ideas were prevalent during the period of the story? Does the author deal with these ideas through his characters? (2f)

The people that braved the trail were a hardy breed. They knew the value of honest work and esteemed perseverance and individual industry. They were accustomed to want and deprivation and considered these troubles the necessary cost of freedom and prosperity.

NOTES:

_____

_____

_____

_____

_____

QUESTIONS ABOUT STRUCTURE: CHARACTERS

Who is the story about? (3)

The main character (protagonist) is the narrator's father, Daddy, who leads his family across the US to the Oregon territory. Delicious, the narrator, is his oldest daughter.

Is the character sane or crazy? (3e)

While onlookers consider Delicious's daddy to be downright crazy, she sees him as a dreamer whose diligence and determination make his success a certainty.

Is the character kind, gentle, stern, emotional, harsh, logical, rational, and compassionate or exacting…? Make up a list of adjectives that describe the protagonist. (3f)

Adjectives describing Daddy include:

brave	determined
daring	harried
ingenuous	diligent
entrepreneurial	a risk-taker
visionary	a dreamer
"sweet as a peach"	

What does the character do for a living? Is he a professional, or a blue-collar worker? Is he wealthy or impoverished? Is he content with his lot in life, or does he long to improve himself? (3h)

Daddy farms fruit for a living. While he loves his work, he hopes to improve his lot by relocating his orchard to Oregon. He'll take fruit to the west.

What do other characters think or say about him? (3k)

Other characters, fellow travelers on the trail, think Daddy is crazy. "When they saw us and all our little fruit trees fluttering in the breeze, they burst out laughing. 'Those leaves will be brown as dirt before you hit the plains.'…'That nursery wagon won't make it halfway across the river.'"

Is the character a member of any particular religious or social group? If so, what do you know about this group? What motivates this group? What do its members feel to be important? (3l)

Daddy is a member of two social groups. He is the leader and head of a family. As such, he bears the weight of responsibility for provision. In addition, he is a pioneer, a term that signifies courage, work ethic, endurance, and vision.

What does the protagonist think is the most important thing in life? How do you know this? Does the protagonist say this out loud, or do his thoughts and actions give him away? (3m)

For Daddy, the most important thing in life is safely transplanting his "babies" – the nursery of fruit trees he hauls – in the soft and pleasant soil of Oregon. Both his words and his actions bear this out throughout the story.

Who else is the story about? (4)

Accompanying Daddy on the trail are Momma, the children, Delicious, the nursery (Daddy's "babies"), other pioneer families, and Nature with her elements.

Is there a single character (or a group of characters) that opposes the protagonist in the story? (4a)

Nature poses the greatest obstacles to Daddy and Delicious. Nature is often personified in the story as a malevolent force seeking to deter Daddy from his objective and to destroy his precious cargo.

NOTES:

_____

_____

_____

_____

_____

_____

_____

_____

QUESTIONS ABOUT STRUCTURE: CONFLICT AND PLOT

What does the protagonist want? (5)

More than anything else, Daddy and Delicious want to successfully transport their orchard across country to Oregon and establish a new orchard.

Does he attempt to overcome something – a physical impediment, or an emotional handicap? (5b) Does he strive to overcome a physical obstacle outside of himself? (5c)

In order to accomplish their goals, Daddy and Delicious must overcome both the negative, discouraging comments of fellow travelers and the natural elements they encounter on the trail.

Is the conflict an external one, having to do with circumstances in the protagonist's physical world, or is it an internal conflict, taking place in his mind and emotions? (5e)

These obstacles represent both internal and external conflict.

Why can't the protagonists have what they want? (6) Do physical or geographical impediments stand in their way? (6a)

Not only do physical/geographical impediments stand in their way (the Platte River, the mountains of Nebraska and Wyoming, etc), but also the natural elements attached to those places during the seasons they encounter. They endure wind, hail, drought, and frost on the trail.

Are the protagonists racing against time? (6e)

As a result of Nature's opposition, the characters race against time, striving to cover the distance before winter arrives.

What kind of conflict is represented in the story? (6g-i)

This is primarily a Man vs. Nature conflict. In addition, however, the naysayers cause a Man vs. Man / Man vs. Self conflict as Daddy and Delicious must endure the taunts without giving way to retaliation or discouragement.

What happens in the story? (8)

- Daddy builds a nursery on wheels. They cross a river, and narrowly escape capsizing.

- They endure a wind and hail storm, shielding the plants with their own clothing.

- They survive drought when they fortuitously discover water in their lost boots on the trail.

- They scale mountains and geographical obstacles by sheer determination and teamwork.

- They fight Jack Frost by watchfully tending a fire throughout the chilly nights.

- Finally, they navigate the great Columbia River, harnessing its energy to work for them by turning their nursery on wheels into a boat.

What events form the climax or highest point of tension in the story? (9)

Delicious's fight against Frost constitutes the climax of the story. This is the final obstacle on the trip.

Does the protagonist solve his own dilemma? Is it solved by some external source or 3rd party? Is he helpless in the end to achieve his goal (like Frodo in Lord of the Rings), or does he triumph by virtue of his own efforts (Odysseus in The Odyssey)? (9e)

After floating the trees downriver, Daddy plants them in the good Oregon dirt. The family overcomes their obstacles through cooperation.

How does the story end? (10) How are the loose ends tied up? How does the solution of the conflict affect each individual character? (10a, d)

As a result of their hard work, the family makes its fortune in fruit. Daddy calls Delicious the "apple of his eye," rewarding her with a new pair of boots! She calls him a "peach."

Does the ending or resolution of the story make any kind of judgments? (10e)

The family's success underscores the rewards of industry and single-minded vision.

NOTES:

_____

_____

_____

QUESTIONS ABOUT STRUCTURE: THEME

What is the main idea of the story? (13)

The story applauds values such as bravery, cooperation, perseverance, single-mindedness, industry, family, the fruits of labor, and diligence. These are at the "core" of the story.

QUESTIONS ABOUT STYLE

Does the author use the sounds of our language to create interest in his story? (14)

Alliteration (14e)

Thicker than Momma's muskrat stew…and muddier…

Fruit trees flutterin'

Daddy's dainties

Peaches are plummeting… plums are plunging…babies go belly-up

Does the author use descriptions and comparisons to create pictures in the reader's mind? (Imagery)(16)

Simile (16d)

Daddy is sweet as a peach – simile

Personification (16e)

Clouds stomping

Wind threw

Jack Frost

Metaphor (16h, 16i)

The wagon is a Prairie schooner

The wagon is a Nursery wagon

The plants are babies

They lived to a ripe old age (parents as fruits)

Delicious is the apple of his eye

Does the author use the characters and events in his story to communicate a theme that goes beyond them in some way? (17)

Allusions (17f)

Reference to the poison apple the old witch gave to Snow White

Naming of real landmarks such as Courthouse Rock and Chimney Rock

NOTES:

_____

_____

_____

_____

_____

_____

_____

_____

_____

_____

_____

QUESTIONS ABOUT CONTEXT

Who is the author? (18)

Deborah Hopkinson is the winner of the Golden Kite Award for picture book text and winner of the Spur storytelling award. She is an Oregon Book Award finalist and a winner of the ALA Notable Book distinction. She writes historical fiction for children from her home in Walla Walla, Washington, where she works as a director for Whitman College. She is mother to two grown children. Her other notable books include *Fannie in the Kitchen* (a biography of famed cookbook author, Fannie Farmer), *A Pocket of Seeds, Saving Strawberry Farm*, and *Sky Boys* (a biography of the workers who erected the Empire State Building).

NOTES:

_____

_____

_____

_____

_____

_____

_____

_____

_____

_____

STORY CHARTS

The following pages contain story charts of the type presented in the live seminar *Teaching the Classics.* As is made clear in that seminar, a separate story chart may be constructed for each of the conflicts present in a work of fiction. In particular, the reader's decision as to the ***climax*** and central ***themes*** of the plot structure will depend upon his understanding of the story's central ***conflict***. As a result, though the details of setting, characters, exposition, and conclusion may be identical from analysis to analysis, significant variation may be found in those components which appear down the center of the story chart: Conflict, Climax, and Theme. This of course results from the fact that literary interpretation is the work of active minds, and differences of opinion are to be expected – even encouraged!

For the teacher's information, one story chart has been filled in on the next page. In addition, a blank chart is included to allow the teacher to examine different conflicts in the same format.

Apples to Oregon by Deborah Hopkinson: Story Chart

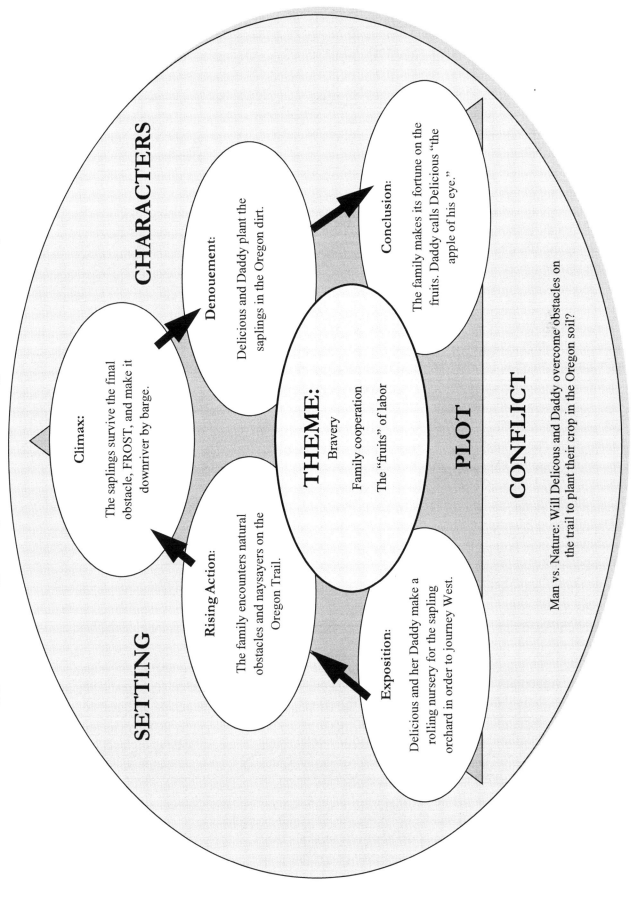

CHARACTERS

SETTING

CONFLICT

PLOT

Climax:

The saplings survive the final obstacle, FROST, and make it downriver by barge.

Denouement:

Delicious and Daddy plant the saplings in the Oregon dirt.

Conclusion:

The family makes its fortune on the fruits. Daddy calls Delicious "the apple of his eye."

THEME:

Bravery

Family cooperation

The "fruits" of labor

Rising Action:

The family encounters natural obstacles and naysayers on the Oregon Trail.

Exposition:

Delicious and her Daddy make a rolling nursery for the sapling orchard in order to journey West.

Man vs. Nature: Will Delicous and Daddy overcome obstacles on the trail to plant their crop in the Oregon soil?

Apples to Oregon by Deborah Hopkinson: Blank Story Chart

CHARACTERS

SETTING

CONFLICT

PLOT

THEME:

Climax:

Denouement:

Conclusion:

Rising Action:

Exposition:

William Steig's
Brave Irene

Questions for Socratic Discussion
by Missy Andrews

CENTER FOR LIT

TABLE OF CONTENTS:
BRAVE IRENE

QUICK CARD

Reference	*Brave Irene* by William Steig ISBN-10: 0374409277 ISBN-13: 978-0374409272
Plot	While her seamstress mother lies ill in bed, little Irene braves a snowstorm to deliver the duchess's finished ball gown in time for the evening's festivities.
Setting	A snowy, windy winter day in the country. A day in the childhood of Irene Bobbin.
Characters	• Irene – a precocious child whose fierce determination and love for her mother drive her to daring deeds of accomplishment; • Mrs. Bobbin – a sick seamstress with a remarkable daughter; • The Duchess – a courtly lady who has hired Mrs. Bobbin to create a beautiful ball gown for a party; • The Doctor and the servants; • The Wind – the antagonist in the story, the personified voice of this element screams, tormenting and toying with Irene, impeding her progress.
Conflict	Man vs. Nature: From the ailment that initially provokes Irene to embark on her errand, to the windy, snowy, dark, and cold elements she battles on the way, the main character, Irene, jousts with nature.
Theme	Diligence and courage have their rewards. "Whatsoever you do, do it with all your heart" (Col. 3:23).
Literary Devices	Alliteration Imagery Simile Personification

QUESTIONS ABOUT STRUCTURE: SETTING

What is the mood or atmosphere of the place where the story happens? Is it cheerful and sunny, or dark and bleak? What words or phrases or descriptions does the author use to create this atmosphere? (1d) What is the weather like in the story? (1e) Among what kinds of people is the story set? What is their economic class? How do they live? Are they hopeful? Downtrodden? Depressed? Why? (1h)

The story is set in the countryside of a kingdom ruled by a monarch. The mood of the story is turbulent and troubled, but not all dark because the main character's attitude is full of determined courage. Although beset by temporary trouble, Irene never wavers in her decisive confidence.

On what day does the story happen? What time of day? (2a)

The story happens on the day the great ball is to be held at the palace.

How long a period of time does the story cover? A few minutes? A single day? A whole lifetime? (2b)

It takes place over the course of a 24-hour period.

In what season does the story take place? (2c)

The events take place in the dead of winter and during a particularly bad blizzard.

In what time of life for the main characters do the events occur? Are they children? Are they just passing into adulthood? Are they already grownups? Does setting the story in this particular time of the characters' lives make the story better? (2e)

The circumstances are intensified by the main character's youth. Perhaps an adult is a match for nature's worst elements, but a young girl is not.

In what intellectual period is the story set? What ideas were prevalent during the period of the story? Does the author deal with these ideas through his characters? Do the characters respond to social rules and customs that are the result of these ideas? (2f)

Since this story is set in a monarchy, the loyalty of subjects to royalty is assumed.

QUESTIONS ABOUT STRUCTURE: CHARACTERS

Who is the story about? (3)

The story's main character is Irene Bobbin.

How old is the protagonist? (3b)

She is perhaps 10-12 years old, a "small person."

Is the character kind, gentle, stern, emotional, harsh, logical, rational, and compassionate or exacting…? Make up a list of adjectives that describe the protagonist. What words or actions on the protagonist's part make you choose the adjectives you do? (3f)

Irene is driven to face the blizzard because of her love and concern for her mother. Her actions prove her a loyal, devoted, responsible, and honest character. While daunted by fear and failure, she perseveres to complete her errand, opposing the wind and elements. She proves herself daring, determined, and trustworthy.

What does the character do for a living? Is she a professional, or a blue-collar worker? Is she wealthy or impoverished? (3h)

Irene is a seamstress's daughter.

What do other characters think or say about her? (3k)

Other characters call her brave and loving.

Is the character a member of any particular religious or social group? If so, what do you know about this group? What motivates this group? What do its members feel to be important? (3l)

The character is a part of a family, and therefore, is motivated by love and a desire for the mutual good of her mother and herself. She considers keeping her word and caring for her mother to be most important. In addition, Irene is a royal subject. As such, she must serve the duchess.

What does the protagonist think is the most important thing in life? How do you know this? Does the protagonist say this out loud, or do her thoughts and actions give her away? (3m)

In this story, Irene thinks that doing what she has promised her mother is the most important thing in life. She believes that delivering the dress to the duchess is supremely important since it will preserve her mother's reputation.

Do the protagonist's priorities change over the course of the story? In what way? What causes this change? Is it a change for the better, or for the worse? (3n)

Initially, this means delivering the ball gown to the duchess before the ball. Once the gown is lost, she means to report the situation to the duchess in person rather than by her absence.

Is the protagonist a sympathetic character? Do you identify with him and hope he will succeed? Do you pity him? Do you scorn or despise his weakness in some way? Why? (3q)

Irene is certainly a sympathetic character. The reader pities her setbacks and cheers her courage and victory.

Who else is the story about? (4)

Other characters include Mrs. Bobbin, the duchess, the doctor, the servants, and the Wind.

Is there a single character (or a group of characters) that opposes the protagonist in the story? (4a)

Of all of these other characters, the Wind is most important as it opposes Irene in her objectives. In this way the Wind, personified, becomes the antagonist. While all of Nature opposes Irene, it is the Wind that gives voice to this antagonism.

In what way is he antagonistic? What goal of the protagonist is he opposed to? (4b)

The Wind opposes Irene's desire to deliver the gown to the Duchess on foot.

What actions does he take to oppose the protagonist? (4c)

The Wind torments and toys with Irene, first heckling her and impeding her progress, then wresting the cherished gown from her grasp.

How does the author's description of the character inform you of his antagonism? Does he have any physical attributes or personality traits that mark him as antagonistic? (4e)

The author personifies the Wind, giving him a voice that screams at Irene, "Go HOOME!" The Wind drives Irene rudely. The Wind blocks her way. It threatens Irene, "Go home, or else." It wrestles her for her package. Finally, it steals the package. Steig describes the Wind as "ill-tempered" and compares it to a "wild animal." Although the Wind races Irene to the finish, she bests it in the end, and the Wind admits defeat with a graceful flourish.

Why does he oppose the protagonist? Does he merely belong to a different social group? Does he see the world in slightly different ways? Or is he an evil villain, like Shakespeare's Iago? (4f)

Nature opposes Irene because of its "ill-temper." It's not personal.

Is the antagonist truly evil, by definition, or is he merely antagonistic to the protagonist by virtue of his vocation or duty? (4m)

The Wind behaves in a way consistent with his nature. He is, in a sense, doing his job, blowing in a blizzard. Likewise, he simultaneously functions as a spur to Irene's nature, bringing out her better character qualities by necessity.

NOTES:

_____

_____

_____

_____

_____

_____

_____

_____

_____

_____

_____

QUESTIONS ABOUT STRUCTURE: CONFLICT AND PLOT

What does the protagonist want? (5)

Irene wants to deliver her mother's newly finished gown to the duchess before the ball so that her mother can rest in both body and mind.

Does he attempt to overcome something – a physical impediment, or an emotional handicap? (5b)

To do so, Irene must overcome the elements: wind, cold, snow, distance, darkness, fear, and her own failure.

Is the conflict an external one, having to do with circumstances in the protagonist's physical world, or is it an internal conflict, taking place in his mind and emotions? (5e)

Although the conflict begins as an external man vs. nature conflict, as the story progresses, the battle becomes more personal and more intense. Irene must master not only the elements, but also herself to arrive at her destination.

Why can't the protagonist have what she wants? (6) Do physical or geographical impediments stand in the protagonist's way? (6a)

Irene must overcome physical and geographical impediments to reach her objective. In particular, she must best the wind, snowdrifts, cold, darkness, and a sprained ankle.

Does the protagonist lack strength, mental acumen or some other necessary ability? (6b)

Irene's lack of physical strength poses an obstacle.

Is the protagonist racing against time? (6e)

Time runs short, as the dress must be delivered before the ball begins.

What kind of conflict is represented in the story? (6g-k)

All these things represent a man vs. nature conflict. There is also a man vs. self conflict here, as Irene must resist discouragement at her setbacks and press on in spite of them.

What other problems are there in the story? (7)

Because of the blizzard, Irene is unable to return home after delivering the dress. She must spend the night at the palace with no means of sending word to her mother. When Mrs. Bobbin wakes in the morning to mountains of snow and no Irene, she is dismayed.

What happens in the story? (8)

- As a result of Mrs. Bobbin's illness, Irene sets out with the dress.

- As a result of the unwieldy package, the Wind is able to wrest it from her.

- As a result of the Wind's impediments and thievery, Irene must go empty-handed to the palace.

- As a result of the deep snow and extreme cold, Irene twists her ankle.

- As a result of the darkness, Irene fears both being alone and missing the ball.

- As a result of her fall into the drift, she is enraged and finds strength to outwit and best her opponent the Wind.

How is the main problem solved? (9)

By determined perseverance, courage, and character, Irene solves her problem. She will not be denied!

How are the protagonist's obstacles finally overcome? (9b) Is the situation pleasantly resolved, or is it resolved in a terrible way? (9c)

When she races the Wind on the box-turned-sled and finds the dress clinging to a tree trunk, Irene is finally victorious.

What events form the highest point or climax of the story's tension? Are they circumstantial events, or emotional ones? Is the climax a spiritual or physical one? (9d)

Irene's final fall into the snow bank marks the climax of the story. She is swallowed up by the weather, her opponent. It can't get worse. However, thoughts of her mother's love spur her forward to the finish line, just as these same thoughts caused her to embark on her journey initially. This is both a physical and an emotional victory.

How does the story end? (10)

Irene's struggle has a happy ending. She accomplishes all she set out to do. The duchess is pleased by the dress, startled to receive it in such bad weather, and impressed by Irene's strength of character. Irene's mother is relieved that all ends well. Irene is satisfied with her accomplishment.

QUESTIONS ABOUT STRUCTURE: THEME

What does the protagonist learn? (11) Is she ennobled in some way? (11c)

The protagonist is ennobled. Irene chooses to go on despite her setbacks and learns to overcome adversity through determination and perseverance.

She realizes her love for her mother: "And never see her mother's face again? Her good mother who smelled like fresh-baked bread?"

What do the other characters learn? (12)

The duchess and her retinue are challenged by Irene's stance towards difficulties. They are impressed by her unflinching willingness to face the elements to honor her family's word.

What is the main idea of the story? (13)

The story's themes include the value of perseverance, fortitude, endurance, courage, determination, and integrity.

NOTES:

_____

_____

_____

_____

_____

_____

_____

QUESTIONS ABOUT STYLE

Does the author use the sounds of our language to create interest in his story? (14)

Alliteration (14e)

<u>w</u>ind <u>wh</u>irled

<u>f</u>lakes were <u>f</u>alling

Does the author use descriptions and comparisons to create pictures in the reader's mind? (16)

Imagery

"The ball gown flounced out and went waltzing through the powdered air with tissue paper attendants." (Metaphor in which the ball gown is compared to the dancing duchess and the tissue paper is compared with her attendants.)

Similes (16d)

"The wind was howling like a wild animal."

"The box shot forward, like a sled."

"The duchess in her new gown was like a bright star in the sky."

Personification (16e) –

Personification is a literary device by which an author lends human characteristics or attributes to an inanimate object or idea. Using this device, authors make tea kettles sing, birds praise their Creator, and flowers dance. Of course, neither kettles, birds, nor flowers participate in the rational life that yields such willful action. However, once the comparison is drawn, the objects become alive and leap off the page in three-dimensional brilliance.

Man against Nature is a common literary theme. Jack London and other Naturalists made it the subject of the bulk of their work. But the unspoken, malevolent force of nature in London's stories takes on new voice and character when imbued by author William Steig with human attributes and personality.

Steig's Wind is a devilish sort of brute. Seeing a small, yet determined girl on a seemingly impossible errand, it endeavors to deter her by presenting obstacle after obstacle. Unruly and unfeeling, the prankster Wind plays a game of tug-of-war for the contents of Irene's parcel. It roughs her up, pushing and pulling at her. Snatching at the precious package, it rips it forcefully from her hands. Then proudly, like a bad winner, the Wind parades the contents of the box on the air before her, seemingly trying its ill-gotten gain on for size before whisking it out of sight, and with it her hopes.

Even so, the protagonist's mettle is not broken, but rather forged by the conflict she encounters. Though the Wind continues to torment the girl, heckling her with its jeers and harassing her with its ferocity, Irene's dauntless character drives her to deliver a message in the stead of the lost package. The Wind roars at her, while she trudges boldly ahead in defiance of its attempts to terrorize her: "Go hoooome. Irene, go hoooooooome!" Still she struggles on through the fierce snowdrifts the Wind lays in her path in the face of great cold, darkness, and loneliness.

Consequently, Irene's fiercely loyal and bold nature is revealed by the antics of the antagonistic Wind. When the prankster returns the stolen article in the final pages of the narrative, his gentler side is revealed. This is no malicious, malevolent entity, but a playful, mischievous adversary. Having found its opponent worthy, it rewards her with the stolen object she cherished as a sort of truce. In effect, the Wind breathes, "All right, Irene. I give. You're a good sport." Having had its fun, the Wind retreats into a calm stillness punctuated by Irene's peaceful sleep and the white blanket of snow across which she is carried home.

In this manner, author William Steig uses personification to develop a man against nature conflict that drives his story forward to a feverish climax before resolving in a gentle breeze of lingering confidence, highlighting the character development of his protagonist.

NOTES:

_____

_____

_____

_____

_____

_____

_____

QUESTIONS ABOUT CONTEXT

Who is the author? (18)

William Steig is the well-known author and illustrator of 25 acclaimed children's classics including *Brave Irene, Amos and Boris*, and *Sylvester and the Magic Pebble*. However, few are aware that his success in the field of children's books represents only his second professional career. Mr. Steig's artistic talents were first recognized and popularized by *The New Yorker* magazine where he served as a cartoonist for 60 years. His interest in children's books began at a colleague's prompting when he was 61 years of age. When asked about his books, he stated that he used animal characters intentionally to symbolize human behavior.

Brooklyn-born to Polish Jewish immigrants, Mr. Steig became an artist at his father's request. A socialist, the elder Steig taught his children that they should take careers neither as businessmen, since they exploit their workers, nor as laborers, since they become exploited. Art was the field of his choosing. Dutifully, William took his father's advice, attending City College for two years and the National Academy for three years. He spent a mere five days at Yale School of Fine Arts. When questioned, he remarked that his own education was "defective." When the depression left his parents (a seamstress and house painter) jobless, William took on the role of provider. Shopping his cartoons, he sold several to *The New Yorker* magazine, which subsequently became his lifelong employer.

In addition to his cartoons and children's books, Mr. Steig popularized both the contemporary greeting card and carved wooden figurines. Steig was the husband of Elizabeth Mead, sister of anthropologist Margaret Mead. Before he died at the age of 95, Mr. Steig encouraged his three children never to take 9-5 jobs, but to spend their lives as artists.

NOTES:

_____

_____

_____

_____

STORY CHARTS

The following pages contain story charts of the type presented in the live seminar *Teaching the Classics*. As is made clear in that seminar, a separate story chart may be constructed for each of the conflicts present in a work of fiction. In particular, the reader's decision as to the **climax** and central **themes** of the plot structure will depend upon his understanding of the story's central **conflict**. As a result, though the details of setting, characters, exposition, and conclusion may be identical from analysis to analysis, significant variation may be found in those components which appear down the center of the story chart: Conflict, Climax, and Theme. This of course results from the fact that literary interpretation is the work of active minds, and differences of opinion are to be expected – even encouraged!

For the teacher's information, one story chart has been filled in on the next page. In addition, a blank chart is included to allow the teacher to examine different conflicts in the same format.

Brave Irene by William Steig: Story Chart

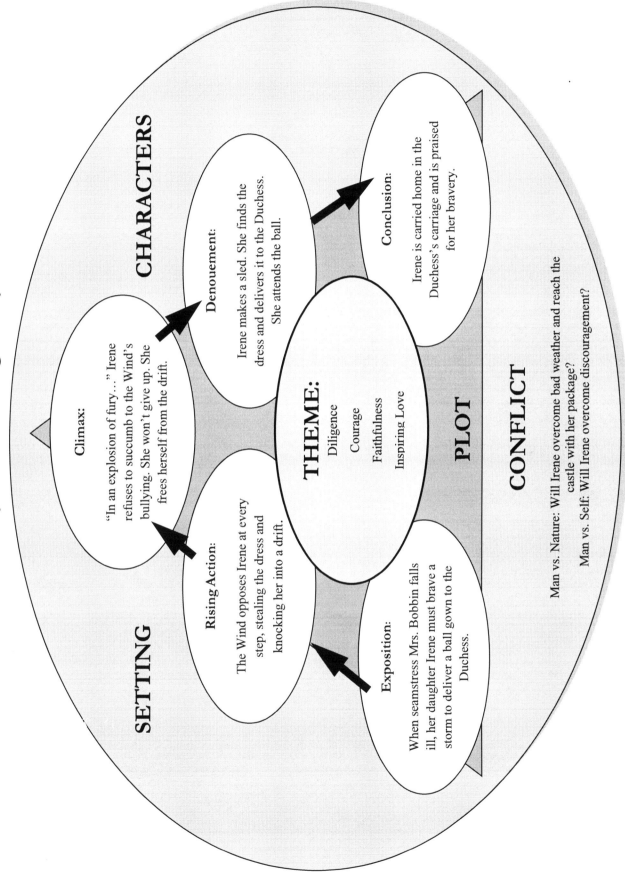

CHARACTERS

SETTING

Climax:
"In an explosion of fury…" Irene refuses to succumb to the Wind's bullying. She won't give up. She frees herself from the drift.

Denouement:
Irene makes a sled. She finds the dress and delivers it to the Duchess. She attends the ball.

Conclusion:
Irene is carried home in the Duchess's carriage and is praised for her bravery.

THEME:
Diligence
Courage
Faithfulness
Inspiring Love

Rising Action:
The Wind opposes Irene at every step, stealing the dress and knocking her into a drift.

Exposition:
When seamstress Mrs. Bobbin falls ill, her daughter Irene must brave a storm to deliver a ball gown to the Duchess.

PLOT

CONFLICT

Man vs. Nature: Will Irene overcome bad weather and reach the castle with her package?

Man vs. Self: Will Irene overcome discouragement?

Brave Irene by William Steig: Blank Story Chart

CHARACTERS

SETTING

Climax:

Rising Action:

Denouement:

THEME:

Conclusion:

Exposition:

PLOT

CONFLICT

Cynthia Rylant's
The Relatives Came

Questions for Socratic Discussion
by Missy Andrews

CENTER FOR LIT

TABLE OF CONTENTS:
THE RELATIVES CAME

QUICK CARD

Reference	*The Relatives Came* by Cynthia Rylant ISBN-10: 0874995329 ISBN-13: 978-0689717383
Plot	When relatives from Virginia descend upon the narrator's family home, they invade his personal space. Yet, when they depart, he finds the house too empty and quiet, making him anticipate their next visit.
Setting	Summer vacation A family
Characters	The narrator, a child (this is a first person narration) An extended family
Conflict	Man vs. Man: The chaos that extended family visits bring. Close spaces.
Theme	When the relatives arrive, the house bursts with joy and activity. The hugging and laughing and eating that ensue are as exhausting as they are wonderful. Things are broken and fixed again. Fruit is harvested, and stories are told. Author Cynthia Rylant evokes vivid recollections of family reunions in *The Relatives Came*. Simultaneously recalling the joys and discomforts of family visits through the childish, honest eyes of the narrator, she captures both the warmth of family relationships and the difficulty of close quarters. Her colorful recap leaves readers longing for the next visit right along with the narrator.

QUESTIONS ABOUT STRUCTURE: SETTING

Where does this story happen? (1)

The story takes place at a country home north of Virginia during an extended family reunion. The presence of school-aged children and ripe fruits suggest summer. The house is too small to accommodate everyone, so they crowd in. The atmosphere is loving, communicative, and festive. The pages burst with the sounds of multiple, simultaneous conversations and activities. These characters aren't wealthy, but they are eager to share what they have with one another.

NOTES:

_____

_____

_____

_____

_____

_____

_____

_____

_____

_____

QUESTIONS ABOUT STRUCTURE: CHARACTERS

Who is the story about? (3)

> There is no single protagonist. The story is told in the first person by one of the children in the family receiving visitors. The narrator's voice is not intrusive. He is one of the members of his immediate family, recalling the wild and wonderful visit. No names are ever mentioned.

Is the character a member of any particular religious or social group? If so, what do you know about this group? What motivates this group? What do its members feel to be important? (3l)

> The character is a member of a social group – his family.

What does the protagonist think is the most important thing in life? How do you know this? Does the protagonist say this out loud, or do his thoughts and actions give him away? (3m)

> Most important to this group is spending time with one another. This is clear since the immediate family of the narrator is willing and happy to do without privacy, personal space, peace, quiet, and their harvest to have their extended relatives come stay for a while.

Who else is the story about? (4)

> The extended family, the relatives, are noisy, boisterous, demonstrative, helpful, and warm. They aren't antagonistic to the main character. They love him. The underlying conflict in the story is the chaos that they bring into the peaceful home during their stay.

NOTES:

_____

_____

_____

_____

_____

QUESTIONS ABOUT STRUCTURE: CONFLICT AND PLOT

What does the protagonist want? (5)

When the relatives are away, the family wants to see them. When they are present, they wish for quiet and peace again. The nature of the conflict takes care of itself.

Why can't he have it? (6)

The conflict is both Man vs. Man (too crowded, too noisy) and Man vs. Nature (spatial separation). While the first conflict will be resolved when the family returns to their home far away, the second will remain. It's this underlying conflict of separation that drives the story. The story itself bridges the underlying conflict. These simultaneous conflicts create a pleasant tension that make both the visit and the time between visits easier to bear.

What happens in the story? (8)

Relatives drive up from Virginia. They descend on the narrator's family, eat up their food, take up their personal space, breathe, help, hug, and laugh.

How is the main problem solved? (9)

The problem is largely solved by the relatives' departure.

What events form the highest point or climax of the story's tension? Are they circumstantial events, or emotional ones? Is the climax a spiritual or physical one? (9d)

When the relatives have eaten up all the strawberries and melons and promised the narrator's family some of their peaches, they pack up and leave.

How does the story end? (10)

The story ends as it began, with more hugging, eating, and breathing, and then a departure. Once the relatives have left, the house seems too big and quiet. Immediately, they miss the relatives and begin planning their next visit.

QUESTIONS ABOUT STRUCTURE: THEME

What is the main idea of the story? (13)

Primary themes in this story include the joy of family relationships and the problem of distance and separation.

Does the story merely call the reader's attention to a theme without trying to solve anything? (13c)

The author doesn't seek to solve the problem she identifies, but just points it out.

How does the story answer the question, "What is a good life?" (13d)

A good life is simply sharing yourself and your blessings with family. It is a life lived in relationships.

NOTES:

_____

_____

_____

_____

_____

_____

_____

_____

_____

_____

QUESTIONS ABOUT CONTEXT

Who is the author? (18)

Author and illustrator Cynthia Rylant was born in West Virginia in 1954. When she was only eight, her parents' divorce necessitated that she live for a time with her grandparents in their Appalachian home. This period of her life became the subject of her first storybook, Caldecott Honor Award winning *When I Was Young in the Mountains*. Miss Rylant, who wrote the book in 1982 during her tenure as a librarian, penned it in only one hour. Getting it published didn't take her much longer, a mere 3 months! This would prove only the first of many notable stories for Miss Rylant. Since then, she has written and published over 100 books for young children, creating such beloved characters as *Henry and Mudge*, *Poppleton*, *Gracie* of the infamous chase, *Mr. Putter*, and *Tabby*. She received a second Caldecott Award in 1985 for *The Relatives Came*, another recollection of her Appalachian childhood. In addition to these awards, Miss Rylant has received both Newbery Awards and Horn/Globe Book Awards.

NOTES:

_____

_____

_____

_____

_____

_____

_____

_____

STORY CHARTS

The following pages contain story charts of the type presented in the live seminar *Teaching the Classics.* As is made clear in that seminar, a separate story chart may be constructed for each of the conflicts present in a work of fiction. In particular, the reader's decision as to the **climax** and central **themes** of the plot structure will depend upon his understanding of the story's central **conflict**. As a result, though the details of setting, characters, exposition, and conclusion may be identical from analysis to analysis, significant variation may be found in those components which appear down the center of the story chart: Conflict, Climax, and Theme. This of course results from the fact that literary interpretation is the work of active minds, and differences of opinion are to be expected – even encouraged!

For the teacher's information, one story chart has been filled in on the next page. In addition, a blank chart is included to allow the teacher to examine different conflicts in the same format.

The Relatives Came by Cynthia Rylant: Story Chart

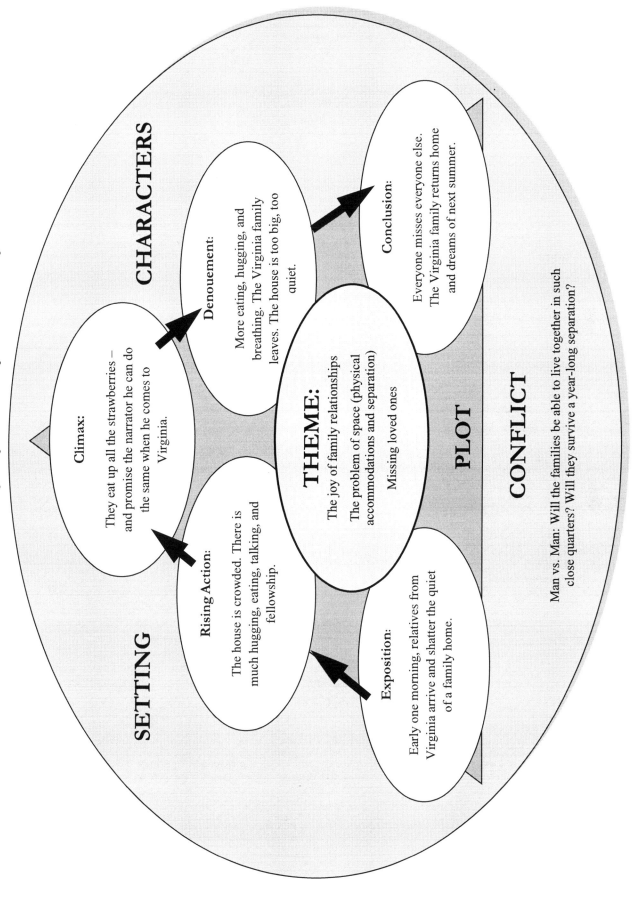

CHARACTERS

Denouement:
More eating, hugging, and breathing. The Virginia family leaves. The house is too big, too quiet.

Climax:
They eat up all the strawberries – and promise the narrator he can do the same when he comes to Virginia.

Conclusion:
Everyone misses everyone else. The Virginia family returns home and dreams of next summer.

THEME:
The joy of family relationships
The problem of space (physical accomodations and separation)
Missing loved ones

Rising Action:
The house is crowded. There is much hugging, eating, talking, and fellowship.

PLOT

CONFLICT

SETTING

Exposition:
Early one morning, relatives from Virginia arrive and shatter the quiet of a family home.

Man vs. Man: Will the families be able to live together in such close quarters? Will they survive a year-long separation?

The Relatives Came by Cynthia Ryland: Blank Story Chart

CHARACTERS

SETTING

CONFLICT

PLOT

THEME:

Climax:

Rising Action:

Denouement:

Conclusion:

Exposition:

Tomie dePaola's
The Clown of God

Questions for Socratic Discussion
by Missy Andrews

CENTER FOR LIT

TABLE OF CONTENTS:
THE CLOWN OF GOD

QUICK CARD

Reference	*The Clown of God* by Tomie dePaola ISBN-10: 0156181924 ISBN-13: 978-0156181921
Plot	An orphaned child establishes himself as a world-class juggler. In time, old age robs him of this place; society no longer wants him. Still, he finds his value in performing for the Lord.
Setting	Sorrento, Italy and the surrounding region during the Renaissance, around 1300-1500.
Characters	• Giovanni – an orphan juggler, the story's namesake • The little brothers of the monastery – monks of the Franciscan order • The players • The audience
Conflict	Man vs. Man Man vs. Himself
Theme	All callings are holy callings. This Giovanni learns from the little brothers of the monastery. When he performs, his performance is an act of service to the most high God. With God he has a place to belong long after the laughter of the audience fades away.
Literary Devices	Repetition Imagery Personification Allusion Foreshadowing Symbolism

QUESTIONS ABOUT STRUCTURE: SETTING

In what country or region does the story happen? (1a)

The story takes place in Sorrento, Italy during the period known as the Renaissance (1300-1500 AD).

Does the story happen in one spot, or does the action unfold across a wide area? (1c)

The action unfolds over a broad space encompassing a variety of towns and audiences throughout Italy. Giovanni performs for both the wealthy and the poor.

Do you long to climb into the pages of the book to live in its world, or does it repel you? Why? (1f) Is the setting of the story important because of historical events which may have taken place there? How does this link help you understand the themes of the story? (1j)

The setting is real and historic. The thematic ideas of the piece stem from ideas of the period.

In what time of life for the main characters do the events occur? Are they children? Are they just passing into adulthood? Are they already grownups? (2e)

The story takes in the lifetime of its main character, Giovanni, but culminates in his old age.

NOTES:

_____

_____

_____

_____

_____

_____

QUESTIONS ABOUT STRUCTURE: CHARACTERS

Who is the story about? (3)

> The protagonist is Giovanni, an orphan juggler who becomes God's clown.

Is the character kind, gentle, stern, emotional, harsh, logical, rational, and compassionate or exacting…? Make up a list of adjectives that describe the protagonist. What words or actions on the protagonist's part make you choose the adjectives you do? (3f)

> Giovanni is a needy child at the story's outset, but discovers a talent within him that makes him useful to the world. He never thinks much of himself, however, nor of his profession.

What do other characters think or say about him? (3k)

> The Little Brothers say that all of Creation sings of the glory of God, including the worldly tasks of common men.

Is the character a member of any particular religious or social group? If so, what do you know about this group? What motivates this group? What do its members feel to be important? (3l)

> Giovanni is member of a traveling acting troupe. They are professional entertainers.

What does the protagonist think is the most important thing in life? How do you know this? Does the protagonist say this out loud, or do his thoughts and actions give him away? (3m)

> Giovanni feels that making people happy is the most important thing. He delights in making others smile.

Is the protagonist a type or archetype? Is he an "Everyman" with whom the reader is meant to identify? Are his struggles symbolic of human life generally in some way? (3p)

> Although readers aren't likely to identify with Giovanni in specifics, they surely will relate to his poverty of spirit, and humility. He is one of the "little ones" mentioned in the Scriptures. Most certainly they will relate to his humanity. As he ages, he loses his physical abilities and is scorned by the world.

Is the protagonist a sympathetic character? Do you identify with him and hope he will succeed? Do you pity him? Do you scorn or despise his weakness in some way? Why? (3q)

As a result, Giovanni is certainly a sympathetic character. Readers pity him in his want and warm to his noble humility.

Who else is the story about? (4)

Other characters include:

The Franciscan Monks – "Little Brothers" whom Giovanni encounters on the open road, and with whom he shares his bread. They, in turn, share wisdom with him.

The Players – entertainers with whom Giovanni initially travels and from whom he learns his trade.

The Audience – fickle folks who warm to Giovanni's greatness and later scorn his weakness.

The Madonna and Child – The statue of Mary and Jesus that affirms Giovanni's gift.

NOTES:

_____

_____

_____

_____

_____

_____

_____

_____

_____

QUESTIONS ABOUT STRUCTURE: CONFLICT AND PLOT

What does the protagonist want? (5)

Initially, Giovanni wants to be useful in order to find a place for himself in society and earn his daily bread. He wants to make people happy. However, as age robs him of his abilities, his usefulness diminishes. He wonders if he still has a place. Community forsakes him. He is discouraged and alone.

Is the conflict an external one, having to do with circumstances in the protagonist's physical world, or is it an internal conflict, taking place in his mind and emotions? (5e)

The conflict, while stimulated from without (the crowd's disapproval and his aging), affects him internally. It's not merely that Giovanni can no longer juggle brilliantly, but that he is no longer of any value to anyone. He is used up and cast aside as refuse by humanity. Discouraged, he gives up juggling forever.

Why can't the protagonist have what he wants? (6) Does the protagonist lack strength, mental acumen or some other necessary ability? (6b)

Giovanni's waning physical strength and faculties prevent him from continuing to serve and delight people.

Does he lack self-confidence, good health, or social connections? (6c)

As a result, Giovanni retreats into himself, certain that he is of no more value to anyone.

What kind of conflict is represented in the story? (6g-l)

Giovanni's troubles represent a Man v. Society, Man v. Himself, and a Man v. God struggle. Society rejects him. He becomes discouraged and defeated. He wonders if he has any remaining value.

Do the protagonist's actions provoke further conflict or unrest in the story? (7b)

Poverty stricken, hungry, sick, and homeless, Giovanni seeks refuge in his hometown church. There he watches the Procession of the Gifts, in which townspeople ceremonially present gifts to a statue of the Madonna and baby Jesus. Dazzled, he too wishes to offer a gift. He proffers all he has – his talent – to the child. Spreading out his mat, he begins to juggle before the child. When the monks see him, they are mortified that he would bring worldly entertainments into the holy sanctuary. Giovanni is completely rapt in his expression of service. Would the Church, too, reject him?

What major events take place in the story as a result of the conflict? (8a)

The clown spends his last strength in honor of the child and falls dead before the statue of the babe. When the friars find Giovanni, they are bewildered to find his golden ball, "the sun in the heavens," in the hands of the newly smiling statue of the Christ child.

Does the protagonist get what he's after? (9a)

The protagonist gets what he's after in three ways. First, he has made the stern statue of the Christ child smile. Second, the smile signifies Christ's blessing on Giovanni's gift, affirming that even his worldly talent could be offered to God. Last, Giovanni has finally found a place for himself. He has gone home to be with his Lord.

What events form the highest point or climax of the story's tension? Are they circumstantial events, or emotional ones? Is the climax a spiritual or physical one? (9d)

The high point of the story occurs when Giovanni juggles for the stern statue of the Christ child. This last performance he offers as a gift to the Lord. It represents both a physical and a spiritual climax. He comes to understand what the Little Brothers had told him so many years before. Everything sings of the glory of God – even his juggling. Giovanni understands his calling and has found his ultimate place, at the feet of the Lord in His service for eternity.

How does the story end? (10) How does the solution of the conflict affect each individual character? (10d)

For Giovanni, all questions are answered. He is at rest in a place all his own. Christ Himself has pronounced his benediction. The two churchmen present are humbled to find that Christ has apparently received the sacrilegious offering of the poor clown.

Does the ending or resolution of the story make any kind of judgments? (10e)

This resolution resoundingly affirms the holiness of all vocations offered to the Lord. All callings are holy callings.

Does the resolution offer any particular perspective or understanding of the story's themes? (10f)

Everything sings of the glory of God.

NOTES:

_____

_____

QUESTIONS ABOUT STRUCTURE: THEME

What does the protagonist learn? (11) Is he ennobled in some way? (11c)

Giovanni is ennobled. When he offers his gift to the Lord, the gift itself is transformed into something holy and important. Simultaneously, Giovanni is changed from cast off beggar to honored heir.

Does he draw upon any motifs or symbols to deepen his explanation of these events? (11f)

That the smiling Christ statue holds in his hands the sun in the heavens poetically affirms not only Giovanni's avocation and gift, but also the Holy Child's lordship over all the stuff of earth.

What do the other characters learn? (12) Do they look at the protagonist differently? (12c)

To the brothers, Giovanni is still a poor clown, but their perspective on his sacrilege is questioned by the authority of the child.

What is the main idea of the story? (13)

Giovanni is a young orphan in Renaissance Italy. Although his life is difficult and his means sparse, his sunny disposition and talent for juggling keep him happy and fed. When an acting troupe comes through his village one day, he is mesmerized. Convinced that he too must become a performer, he peddles his abilities to the Maestro and begins traveling with the troupe. Age and experience hone Giovanni's skills until he is regaled as the finest of performers. No longer does he beg for his bread. He is wealthy and respected.

While traveling across the countryside one day, Giovanni shares his lunch with two Franciscan monks. These men in turn share with him their philosophy that all things sing of the glory of God. When they suggest that his juggling might also do so, Giovanni merely laughs good naturedly and continues his journey.

The simple truth that all things sing the glory of God becomes the theme of author Tomie DePaola's medieval folk tale. While the Catholic church of Giovanni's day created a distinction between the sacred and the secular, Brother Francis (for whom the Franciscan monks are named) taught otherwise. Franciscans rejoiced in the glory God receives when creation and man function in the gifts He gave them. This philosophy also animated Protestant reformers such as Martin Luther, who taught that every occupation is a holy calling.

Giovanni's talent cannot last forever, though. Age debilitates the juggler, robbing him of his skill. When he begins to drop his rainbow of balls during live performances, he becomes aware that his days on the stage are over. Worse, the public that had once befriended and sought after him now jeers and taunts him. Forsaken, Giovanni returns to his home town of Sorrento to beg once more for his bread. After an arduous journey, he collapses in the Catholic Church in town. There he encounters a statue of the Virgin Mary and the baby Jesus. Concerned by the stern countenance of the child, Giovanni decides to put on one last performance, a gift of his talents to the child.

Though the brothers who discover Giovanni's gift are stricken and horrified, God, it would seem, is pleased. The image of the Christ child mystically affirms the holiness of Giovanni's worldly profession and delights in his humble offering. Giovanni's tale and its moving resolution capture the joy and glory of a holy calling, no matter how simple.

While distinctly Catholic in its pageantry and mysticism, the theological content of this story is far broader. It suggests that he who would serve God need not enter a monastery to do so. Rather he may offer his talents to the One who allocated them and receive the joy of an audience that never spurns, ridicules, or despises.

What answer does the story seem to suggest for the question, "What is a good life?" (13d)

Giovanni affirms that a truly good life is one offered in service to God, glorifying Him with one's gifts and abilities.

What aspect of the human condition is brought to light and wondered at in this story? (13e)

This is a wonder – that God would delight in the humble gifts of man. As Psalm 8 says, "When I consider the heavens, the moon and the stars which You have ordained, what is man that You are mindful of him?"

NOTES:

_____

_____

_____

_____

_____

_____

_____

_____

QUESTIONS ABOUT STYLE

Does the author use the sounds of our language to create interest in his story? (14)

Repetition

The repetition of Giovanni's lines in his juggling routine become a familiar device within the story and gain importance at the story's climax.

Does the author use descriptions and comparisons to create pictures in the reader's mind? (16)

Imagery (16a, b)

The author's use of the golden ball to represent the sun in the heavens is a kind of image, as is the "rainbow" of colored balls Giovanni juggles. The image of the golden ball is extended in meaning when the Son of the Heavens deigns to hold it in His hands (symbolism).

Personification (16e)

The statue of the Christ child smiles. The statue is given human – godlike qualities. This is a storytelling device, but also references the mystical miracles to which Catholics attest.

Does the author use the characters and events in his story to communicate a theme that goes beyond them in some way? (17)

Allusion (17f)

The author alludes both to the philosophies of the Franciscan monks and to Catholic doctrines.

Foreshadowing (17a-c)

Giovanni's early encounter with the Franciscan brothers informs his experience at the story's turning point. Whereas his service to earthly audiences proves ultimately vain, his service to the baby King proves his lasting purpose.

Symbolism (17h)

The juggler is a Clown. The clown, himself, embodies poverty of spirit, humanity in all its frailty and weakness. He is an Everyman.

The ball symbolizes the stuff of the earth – rainbows, the sun, etc.

The author inserts doves in most all of his illustrations, alluding to the Holy Spirit and making Him pictorially present throughout the stages of Giovanni's life.

NOTES:

_____

_____

_____

_____

_____

_____

_____

_____

_____

_____

_____

_____

QUESTIONS ABOUT CONTEXT

Who is the author? (18)

Tomie dePaola was born in Meriden, Connecticut, one of three siblings. When he was only four years old, he set his heart upon a career in writing and illustrating books. During his formative years, he spent hours drawing and working in theatrical productions. After graduating from high school, he attended Pratt Institute in Brooklyn, New York.

His schooling complete, he illustrated his first book, *SOUND*. Soon after, he wrote and illustrated *The Wonderful Dragon of Timlin*. Perhaps his most famous books include *26 Fairmont Avenue* and *Meet the Barkers*, both of which won the Newbery Medal. Another of his well-loved favorites is *Strega Nona*, which received a Caldecott Award. Mr. De Paola has sold over 6 million books worldwide and has taught art at the college level for many years. In 40 years, he has published more than 200 books and joyfully continues his work in New London, New Hampshire.

NOTES:

_____

_____

_____

_____

_____

_____

_____

_____

STORY CHARTS

The following pages contain story charts of the type presented in the live seminar *Teaching the Classics*. As is made clear in that seminar, a separate story chart may be constructed for each of the conflicts present in a work of fiction. In particular, the reader's decision as to the **climax** and central **themes** of the plot structure will depend upon his understanding of the story's central **conflict**. As a result, though the details of setting, characters, exposition, and conclusion may be identical from analysis to analysis, significant variation may be found in those components which appear down the center of the story chart: Conflict, Climax, and Theme. This of course results from the fact that literary interpretation is the work of active minds, and differences of opinion are to be expected – even encouraged!

For the teacher's information, one story chart has been filled in on the next page. In addition, a blank chart is included to allow the teacher to examine different conflicts in the same format.

The Clown of God by Tomie dePaola: Story Chart

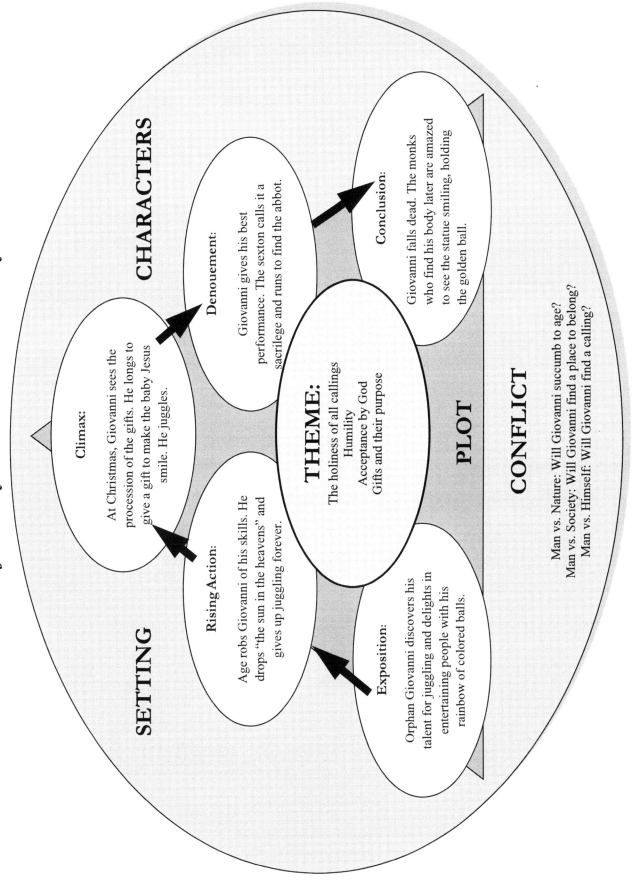

CHARACTERS

SETTING

THEME:
The holiness of all callings
Humility
Acceptance by God
Gifts and their purpose

PLOT

CONFLICT

Man vs. Nature: Will Giovanni succumb to age?
Man vs. Society: Will Giovanni find a place to belong?
Man vs. Himself: Will Giovanni find a calling?

Climax:
At Christmas, Giovanni sees the procession of the gifts. He longs to give a gift to make the baby Jesus smile. He juggles.

Denouement:
Giovanni gives his best performance. The sexton calls it a sacrilege and runs to find the abbot.

Conclusion:
Giovanni falls dead. The monks who find his body later are amazed to see the statue smiling, holding the golden ball.

Rising Action:
Age robs Giovanni of his skills. He drops "the sun in the heavens" and gives up juggling forever.

Exposition:
Orphan Giovanni discovers his talent for juggling and delights in entertaining people with his rainbow of colored balls.

The Clown of God by Tomie dePaola: Blank Story Chart

CHARACTERS

SETTING

CONFLICT

PLOT

THEME:

Climax:

Denouement:

Rising Action:

Conclusion:

Exposition:

Sharon Creech's
Fishing in the Air

Questions for Socratic Discussion
by Missy Andrews

CENTER FOR LIT

TABLE OF CONTENTS:
FISHING IN THE AIR

QUICK CARD

Reference	*Fishing in the Air* by Sharon Creech ISBN-10: 1591122244 ISBN-13: 978-1591122241
Plot	On a fishing trip, a father and his son fish not only for dinner, but also for lost fragments of the past.
Setting	An early morning fishing trip for a father and son. The country, the river, the sky, childhood.
Characters	• The boy and his father (protagonists) • The father's father • Time (the antagonist): "Where is that father/ that boy?"
Conflict	Man vs. Nature: The father, wondering at the passage of time, searches his memory to find his past.
Theme	The passage of time. Memory and family traditions create continuity between generations, overcoming the obstacles of time and aging. The bonds between father and son.
Literary Devices	Imagery Motif/Metaphor – Fishing Similes Alliteration Sensory Language

QUESTIONS ABOUT STRUCTURE: SETTING

In what country or region does the story happen? (1a) Do you long to climb into the pages of the book to live in its world, or does it repel you? Why? (1f)

The story takes place on a father and son fishing trip. It begins before dawn in the early morning and spans a lazy, lovely day. The scene is idyllic. The sky is full of white, puffy clouds. The air is drenched in sunshine. The smell of the river and the sounds of nature surround the pair. The warmth of the place and the relationship the characters share draw readers into their world. The place could be anywhere; its beauty makes it inviting by itself. Still it's the relationship between the characters that makes it singularly attractive.

Is there anything symbolic or allegorical about the place where the story happens? (1i) Is the setting of the story important because of historical events which may have taken place there? How does this link help you understand the themes of the story? (1j)

While there's no direct significance of the place, the setting and event reminds the father of childhood fishing trips with his own dad. This similarity creates a continuity that transcends temporal, physical boundaries between the past and the present, pointing at thematic elements the story will proceed to flesh out.

When does this story happen? (2)

The story covers a single summer day. However, it's set in the spring of the boy's life and the fall of the father's.

NOTES:

_____

_____

_____

_____

_____

_____

QUESTIONS ABOUT STRUCTURE: CHARACTERS

Who is the story about? (3)

> The protagonist of the story (who is also the narrator) is a young boy. He is carefree and content. In contrast to the father, he has no real responsibilities. He's the child in the relationship, enjoying being loved and cared for by a good father.

Is the character a member of any particular religious or social group? If so, what do you know about this group? What motivates this group? What do its members feel to be important? (3l)

> Although he doesn't know it, as a member of his father's family, the boy belongs to a special group of people – his ancestors. He inherits from them not only physical traits, but also character traits, values, and traditions. It seems from the text that family relationships and time together are especially important to these people.

What does the protagonist think is the most important thing in life? How do you know this? Does the protagonist say this out loud, or do his thoughts and actions give him away? (3m)

> The character is really too young to have a developed opinion about the weighty issues of life, but he's learning with every cast of his line the importance of family relationships and time shared together.

Who else is the story about? (4)

> The father is equally important in this story. As the boy "fishes" for a story, the father "bites" and begins remembering his own childhood aloud. His elusive memories create conflict, calling up the lost past. "Where is that father and that boy?" the father pines.

> The subtlety of this conflict can make it difficult to identify. The past times the father recalls make him melancholy, casting shadows in an otherwise sunny scene. The father is the son's world. When clouds gather on his brow, the son's sky darkens. Time, then, is a silent antagonist in this story. Its quiet progress brings change to us and to others. Most often felt when it runs out, time threatens the continuity of family relationships with its stealthy approach.

Why does he oppose the protagonist? Does he merely belong to a different social group? Does he see the world in slightly different ways? Or is he an evil villain, like Shakespeare's Iago? (4f)

Of course, the conflict between the father and time is entirely impersonal. Time works on all men. All men are bound by it. It is a part of the natural world to which all creatures are subject. This conflict underscores the human condition, giving the story universal significance.

NOTES:

_____

_____

_____

_____

_____

_____

_____

_____

_____

_____

_____

_____

_____

QUESTIONS ABOUT STRUCTURE: CONFLICT AND PLOT

What does the protagonist want? (5)

> The son wants to share his father's memories and pursuits. He wants to "catch" something.

Does he attempt to overcome something – a physical impediment, or an emotional handicap? (5b)

> As the son fishes, his father's thoughts are stirred and he ponders his lost and distant past.

Does he strive to overcome a physical obstacle outside of himself (An ocean, for example, like Christopher Columbus, or nature generally, like a Jack London character)? (5c)

> The father strives against Time and Nature. The son remains childishly unaware.

Does the protagonist try to capture an object? (5d)

> The father's object is peace and perspective.

Do his objectives or goals change throughout the story? How? Why? (5f)

> The father's object at the start of the story is a father-son friendship. Yet as his present experience evokes nostalgic memories, he wrestles with his melancholy.

Why can't he have it? (6) What kind of conflict drives this story forward? (6h)

> The conflict is a Man vs. Nature struggle.

What happens in the story? (8)

- The father and son get up early and hop in the car for a fishing trip.

- The boy enjoys the early morning hours before the sun rises, and wonders at the sights and sounds around him.

- Arriving at the river, sun shining gloriously, the two find their spot and begin to fish.

- While the father fishes, the son casts his hookless bobber into the air again and again.

- The surroundings and activity remind the father of his boyhood fishing trips with his own father.

How is the main problem solved? (9) What events form the highest point or climax of the story's tension? Are they circumstantial events, or emotional ones? Is the climax a spiritual or physical one? (9d)

The climax of the story occurs as the father wonders where that remembered boy and father went. His son, however, "catches" what he's fishing for in an instant of childish literalism:

"Where is that father and that son?" "'Right here,' I said."

The boy "finds" the lost pair in himself and his dad. For the father, the son's words produce an epiphany. He sees his past in his present experience and realizes that his father lives on in him, in a sense. In this way, the father discovers the power of shared traditions to create continuity between generations.

How does the story end? (10)

The story comes full circle as the two embrace and trek home with their "catch," content with the world and each other, connected with their ancestors, and shored up by their shared experience.

NOTES:

_____

_____

_____

_____

_____

_____

_____

QUESTIONS ABOUT STRUCTURE: THEME

What is the main idea of the story? (13)

In Sharon Creech's poetic children's story, *Fishing In the Air*, a young boy accompanies his father on an early morning fishing trip. Leaving the light-lined city streets for the open spaces of the country, the two revel in the magical pleasures of nature which are heightened all the more by the boy's active imagination. Imagery abounds as the boy perceives moons in lamplight, rows of soldiers at attention in the tall pines that line the road, and angelic choirs in the warbling of birds.

While the father fishes, the boy casts his hookless fishing line high into the air and plies his father with questions. These and the lazy river evoke from the father bright memories of the past that swim before him elusively. Still the boy baits his father, and still the ephemeral images waver as the father is swept away by nostalgia and begins asking his own questions. "Where is that father, and where is that boy?" he ponders.

As the boy casts one final time, he "catches it all" – he sees in the moment his own scene, and in his scene, echoes of his father's childhood. "Right here," he responds.

The father learns the importance of communion and fellowship between generations. The story suggests that a "good life" is one achieved, in part, by giving to one's children what was given to oneself. It suggests that a good life involves sharing family traditions and time with children, creating memories, and building relationships that rob time of its power to rob us.

Creech's beautiful imagery and illustrator Chris Raschka's imaginative art together evoke the deep magic of family traditions and their mystical ability to marry the past and the present. Her story strikes a universal chord in its exploration of the abstract nature of time and the enduring power of family relationships. Her fishing motif powerfully baits readers to share their past with someone in their present for the dual purpose of nurturing both others and self.

NOTES:

_____

_____

_____

QUESTIONS ABOUT STYLE

Does the author use the sounds of our language to create interest in his story? (14)

Alliteration (14e)

"<u>d</u>amp <u>d</u>irt"

"<u>b</u>ubbles of <u>b</u>reeze and <u>b</u>irds"

"<u>r</u>ed <u>r</u>oof and <u>r</u>olling green fields with <u>r</u>ed flowers waving…a <u>r</u>iver <u>r</u>ippling"

Does the author use descriptions and comparisons to create pictures in the reader's mind? (16)

Imagery

"The grass left wet marks on our shoes. In the backyard, under stones, we dug up crawly worms and laid them in a can with lumps of damp dirt."

"There were green fields around it, rolling green fields with bright red flowers here and there like floating rubies…"

Similes (16d)

"Look at those street lamps…glowing like tiny moons all in a row."

"Those trees…don't they look like tall green soldiers standing at attention?"

"…birds singing their songs like little angels"

Red flowers are like floating rubies

Metaphor (16h)

lamps became moons

trees became soldiers

"bubbles of breeze"

"birds became …little angels singing their songs"

By extension and implication, the "air" the boy fishes in is the father's past, time, memories or thoughts. They are ephemeral, abstract, and fleeting.

How does this help create mood for the story? (16j)

The use of metaphors stirs the imagination of the child in the story to create a sense of wonder and magic. In addition, metaphors and imagery stir the father's senses so as to recall memories from his youth, evoking the past.

Personification (16e, f)

trees become soldiers

birds speak with voices of angels

Does the author use the character and events in his story to communicate a theme that goes beyond them in some way? (17)

Irony (17d)

The boy's words, "Here they are…" are ironic; he refers to himself and his father, yet his father sees in them the other boy and father of his memory. The father recognizes that his own father has reproduced himself in him.

Symbolism (17h, i, m)

The boy, the father, and the fishing trip all represent and recall another boy, another father, and another fishing trip from long ago in the father's own childhood.

The fishing trip/special time symbolizes the father's past. This becomes a motif in the story.

The "air" the child fishes in represents time and memory.

NOTES:

_____

_____

_____

_____

_____

_____

QUESTIONS ABOUT CONTEXT

Who is the author? (18)

Author Sharon Creech was born in Ohio in 1945 and was one of five children. She has taught English and composition at a high school boarding school called The American School in Switzerland. She is married to Lyle Rigg, headmaster of the Penington School in New Jersey. Together they have two children, Rob and Karin. Mrs. Creech has written numerous books, two of which have received Newbery Medals. *Fishing in the Air* was published in 2000.

On the subject of fishing, Mrs. Creech confesses a lack of interest in the sport itself. Yet she continues to enjoy the process: the setting, the conversation, the opportunity it creates to build a relationship with a companion.

She writes, "I don't really like fishing…I mean the act of catching fish. What I do love is sitting in a rowboat or on the dock with a fishing rod, casting lazily into the air. To me fishing is more about being outside in a tranquil setting, smelling the air, gazing at the water and the sky. It is also about the small and large exchanges between you and whoever you are with…many of my father's gifts were an appreciation for the outdoors, a way of seeing and smelling and feeling things that you could "catch" and bring home with you and call upon when you needed them."

NOTES:

_____

_____

_____

_____

_____

_____

_____

STORY CHARTS

The following pages contain story charts of the type presented in the live seminar *Teaching the Classics*. As is made clear in that seminar, a separate story chart may be constructed for each of the conflicts present in a work of fiction. In particular, the reader's decision as to the **climax** and central **themes** of the plot structure will depend upon his understanding of the story's central **conflict**. As a result, though the details of setting, characters, exposition, and conclusion may be identical from analysis to analysis, significant variation may be found in those components which appear down the center of the story chart: Conflict, Climax, and Theme. This of course results from the fact that literary interpretation is the work of active minds, and differences of opinion are to be expected – even encouraged!

For the teacher's information, one story chart has been filled in on the next page. In addition, a blank chart is included to allow the teacher to examine different conflicts in the same format.

Fishing in the Air by Sharon Creech: Story Chart

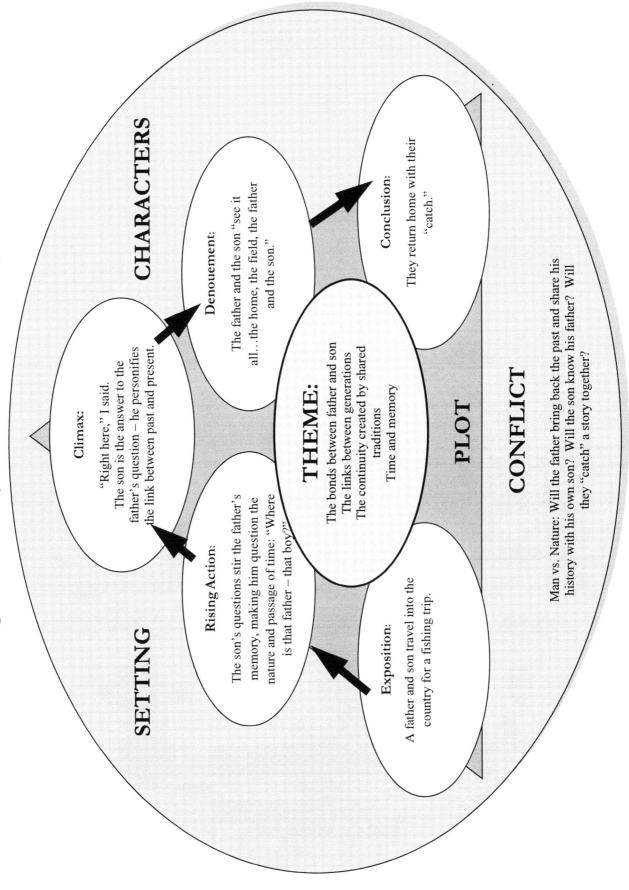

CHARACTERS

SETTING

Climax:
"Right here," I said. The son is the answer to the father's question – he personifies the link between past and present.

Denouement:
The father and the son "see it all…the home, the field, the father and the son."

Conclusion:
They return home with their "catch."

Rising Action:
The son's questions stir the father's memory, making him question the nature and passage of time: "Where is that father – that boy?"

THEME:
The bonds between father and son
The links between generations
The continuity created by shared traditions
Time and memory

PLOT

Exposition:
A father and son travel into the country for a fishing trip.

CONFLICT

Man vs. Nature: Will the father bring back the past and share his history with his own son? Will the son know his father? Will they "catch" a story together?

Fishing in the Air by Sharon Creech: Blank Story Chart

CHARACTERS

SETTING

CONFLICT

PLOT

THEME:

Climax:

Denouement:

Conclusion:

Rising Action:

Exposition:

Mem Fox's
Wilfrid Gordon McDonald Partridge

Questions for Socratic Discussion
by Missy Andrews

CENTER FOR LIT

TABLE OF CONTENTS:
WILFRID GORDON MCDONALD PARTRIDGE

QUICK CARD

Reference	*Wilfrid Gordon McDonald Partridge* by Mem Fox ISBN-10: 091629126X ISBN-13: 978-0916291266
Plot	When Wilfrid learns that his favorite person at the nearby retirement home has lost her memory, he sets out to recover it.
Setting	A neighborhood home situated next door to an assisted living home.
Characters	• Wilfrid Gordon McDonald Partridge (protagonist) – a small, thoughtful child who lives next door to an old folks home. Residents of the retirement home: • Mrs. Jordan – She plays the organ. • Mr. Hoskings – He tells Wilfrid scary stories. • Mr. Tippett – He is "crazy about cricket!" • Miss Mitchell – She has difficulty getting around; Wilfrid runs errands for her. • Mr. Drysdale – Wilfrid is awed by this man's booming voice. • Miss Nancy Alison Delacourt Cooper – Wilfrid's special friend, she always has time for Wilfrid. He is first drawn to her because she has four names, just as he does. When he learns she's losing her memory, Wilfrid is determined to find it again. Other characters: • Wilfrid's parents – They pity Miss Nancy as she loses her memory, but accept it matter of-factly as part of the aging process.
Conflict	Miss Nancy has lost her memory. Wilfrid, who loves his friend, must discover the meaning of "memory" and locate Nancy's. (Man vs. Nature)
Theme	Wilfrid's quest results in a truly heartwarming examination of the meaning attached to special objects, and the value of human kindness. Such kindness knows no age.
Literary Devices	Symbolism- something seen represents something unseen. In this story, the various objects Wilfrid gives Miss Nancy represent memories of things and times in her past.

QUESTIONS ABOUT STRUCTURE: SETTING

Where does this story happen? (1)

The story takes place in a suburban neighborhood where Wilfrid, the main character, lives next door to a retirement home. Wilfrid is a frequent visitor there. The home is full of wonderful people, but none as special as Miss Nancy Alison Delacourt Cooper. Wilfrid's relationship with Miss Nancy fills the story with warmth. The main events of the story's plot take place in just a few hours; yet, they evoke memories of distant years for Nancy.

When does this story happen? In what time of life for the main characters do events occur? Are they children? Are they just passing into adulthood? Are they already grownups? Does setting the story in this particular time of the characters' lives make the story better? (2e)

The characters' ages are very significant factors for this story. Wilfrid's openness, eagerness, simplicity, and earnest *compassion* (all characteristics of youth) are necessary for the story's events to unfold. He is still child enough to believe that Miss Nancy's memory can be found. He has not accepted the permanent effects of aging because he isn't familiar with them. Consequently, he's not bound by his assumptions.

Miss Nancy's age is also significant. Not only does old age bring memory loss, but it also brings lengthened days. Elderly people have time to spend – idle hours to give to children like Wilfrid whose days also stretch out before them. It's this shared time that sparks their friendship – well, this and their long names!

NOTES:

_____

_____

_____

_____

_____

_____

QUESTIONS ABOUT STRUCTURE: CHARACTERS

Who is this story about? (3)

The story's protagonist is young Wilfrid Gordon McDonald Partridge, a small, thoughtful boy, who befriends an elderly lady in a retirement home next door to his house.

How old is the protagonist? (3b)

The narrator tells us that Wilfrid is "not very old, either."

Is the character kind, gentle, stern, emotional, harsh, logical, rational, and compassionate or exacting…? Make up a list of adjectives that describe the protagonist. What words or actions on the protagonist's part make you choose the adjectives you do? (3f)

Wilfrid's actions show that he's a generous soul: compassionate, friendly, sensible, and resourceful. While Wilfrid's age makes him naive, his literal sensibilities allow him to approach Miss Nancy's problem with fresh and engaging perspective. Who says an old person must lose her memories for good? Not Wilfrid. His straightforward and accepting nature, together with his eager and loving heart, compels him to gather objects that will restore to Miss Nancy her lost memories.

What does the protagonist think is the most important thing in life? How do you know this? Does the protagonist say this out loud, or do his thoughts and actions give him away? (3m)

Wilfrid's quiet response to Nancy's trouble communicates his regard for friendship. What's most important to Wilfrid? Whatever his friend most needs. His open, loving nature and childishness make him instantly sympathetic. His collection of memories makes readers smile with a combination of empathetic pity (circumstantial irony) and fondness. Poor Wilfrid, he doesn't know memories aren't shells or medals or eggs. Isn't he cute?

Who else is the story about? (4)

In addition to Wilfrid, there are several other significant characters in the story. These include:

Miss Nancy Alison Delacourt Cooper – Wilfrid's special friend, this resident always has time for him. He is first drawn to her because she has four names, just as he does.

Wilfrid's parents – They pity Miss Nancy for her memory loss, but accept it matter-of-factly as part of the natural aging process.

The other rest home residents whom Wilfrid befriends:

Mrs. Jordan, "who played the organ"

Mr. Hoskings, "who tells scary stories"

Mr. Tippet, "who's crazy about cricket"

Miss Mitchell, "who walks with a cane"

Mr. Drysdale, "who has a voice like a giant"

NOTES:

_____

_____

_____

_____

_____

_____

_____

_____

_____

_____

_____

_____

QUESTIONS ABOUT STRUCTURE: CONFLICT AND PLOT

What does Wilfrid want? (5)

When Wilfrid learns that his favorite friend has lost her memory, he sets out to find it for her again. Of course, unbeknownst to Wilfrid, memory is an abstract concept (5d) rather than a physical object. He asks the other residents of the retirement home to define memory for him, and he does his best to collect the things he supposes them to mean.

Why can't he have it? (6)

Wilfrid's search for Miss Nancy's memory is a Man vs. Nature conflict. Nature in the form of time and old age has robbed Nancy of her memory. Wilfrid's own childish understanding at first seems like a hindrance to his goals of restoring memory to his friend, yet his childish simplicity becomes the vehicle for his discovery.

What happens in the story? (8)

Wilfrid hears that his 96-year-old friend Nancy has lost her memory. He determines to find it for her and asks all her friends what memory is so that he can search for it. (8a,b) Mrs. Jordan tells him memories are warm. Mr. Hoskings tells him they're something old. Mr. Tippet explains that memories make you cry. Miss Mitchell adds that they make you laugh. Mr. Drysdale pronounces them precious as gold. So Wilfrid sets out to collect things matching these descriptions.

How is the main problem solved? (9)

Placing his odd assortment of gathered objects in a basket, Wilfrid delivers them to a bewildered Miss Nancy. As he presents her with each new object, her mind associates the objects with her own past experiences, and her memory is restored. (9d) Wilfrid's presentation of the gift and Miss Nancy's stirred memories form the climax of the story.

How does the story end? (10)

Wilfrid listens eagerly to Nancy's recollected stories. He enjoys the vivid memories of her past almost as much as she does.

How does the solution of the conflict affect each individual character? (10d)

This shared experience validates both Wilfrid and Nancy and make their friendship stronger.

QUESTIONS ABOUT STRUCTURE: THEME

What do the other characters learn? Are other people in the story ennobled, changed, improved or otherwise affected by the story's events? (12a)

Miss Nancy is helped by Wilfrid's childish and generous act. We don't see the final response of other characters, but as he searches out the meaning of memory, the other residents find him strange and sweet.

What is the main idea of the story? (13)

Wilfrid Gordon is a regular visitor at the rest home situated next door to his house. Although he is a small boy, he is welcomed by the residents. Their colorful personalities and scary stories keep him well entertained. One resident in particular, Miss Nancy Alison Delacourt Cooper, becomes his special friend. Since he identifies with her lengthy name, and since she always seems to have time for him, their relationship grows. Unfortunately, Miss Nancy's mind is aging and her memory has begun to fail. This disturbs the child, who straightaway purposes to reclaim it for her.

Having interviewed the other residents concerning the meaning of "memory", Wilfrid begins to collect random objects, each of which are in some way associated with his friends' definitions. These gathered objects become symbols of universal, human experiences, and so prompt Miss Nancy's lagging memory.

A memory is something warm – and so Wilfrid brings a fresh hen egg. A memory is something that makes you cry – and so Wilfrid brings a medal his dead grandfather once gave him. A memory is something that provokes laughter – and so Wilfrid brings his furry puppet on strings. A football that he counts priceless too is taken, along with some old shells from "long ago."

When Miss Nancy sorts through this basket of gatherings, her mind fixes on events in her own life associated with similar objects. A medal makes her think of her soldier brother, lost in a war. The puppet brings back vivid pictures of her laughing little sister. Each object becomes a symbol which evokes recollections of some past experience in Miss Nancy's life. Bit by bit, her memory returns. This symbolism functions as a touchstone between two very different souls, a common language that both can speak.

While young Wilfrid lacks wisdom and maturity, he seems to understand both this universal language of human experience, and the medicinal effects of kindness. Rather than counting his own objects and experiences unique in kind from those of the adults around him, he expects Miss Nancy will see in them the same value as he does. Regardless of their difference in age, Wilfrid Gordon McDonald Partridge and Miss Nancy Alison Delacourt Cooper are really as alike as their names. They're human beings.

Major themes of the story include:

- Friendship across the generations

- The universal nature of human experience – that is, the experience of being a creature on earth

- Kindness

- The transcendent value of the individual apart from age, "usefulness," and knowledge.

- The ingenuity of children – the possibilities that exist when one is unaware of impossibilities.

NOTES:

_____

_____

_____

_____

_____

_____

_____

_____

_____

_____

_____

QUESTIONS ABOUT STYLE

Does the author use the sounds of our language to create interest in his story? (14)

Rhyme (14f):

"He liked Mr. Jordan who played the organ."

"He played with Mr. Tippet who was crazy about cricket."

Understatement

The author describes Wilfrid as a small boy, "who wasn't very old, either…"

In addition to these, the author utilizes repetition, a Hebrew poetic device often used by children's authors.

Does the author use the characters and events in his story to communicate a theme that goes beyond them in some way? (17)

Irony (17d)

Wilfrid's predisposition to interpret everything literally creates a kind of circumstantial irony in the story. The reader understands what Wilfrid does not – that memories are abstract and cannot be collected – and that 96-year-olds' lost memories are seldom found again.

Symbolism (17h,l)

Each of the objects Wilfrid carefully collects represents a memory for Miss Nancy. The warm egg represents her childhood discovery of a blue egg in her aunt's garden. The shell reminds her of a trip she once made to the beach. The medal evokes sad memories of a brother, lost to war. The puppet garners smiles as she remembers her sister, laughing at her own puppet so long ago. Collectively, the objects symbolize the stuff of human experience – creaturehood. It's this shared humanity that facilitates the friendship between Nancy and Wilfrid, in spite of the many years that separate them.

NOTES:

_____

_____

_____

QUESTIONS ABOUT CONTEXT

Who is the author? (18)

Australian born Mem Fox has authored 25 noted children's books. Among these are the heartwarming *Wilfrid Gordon McDonald Partridge* and the swashbuckling *Tough Boris*. Ms. Fox has also authored *Reading Magic*, a book aimed at parents of children aged 0-5 years, and *Radical Reflections: Passionate Opinions on Teaching, Learning and Living*, a teacher's text. In addition to her zeal for teaching teachers, she is actively involved in a literacy campaign, writing what she terms the "literature of liberation…from the tyranny of the attitudes and expectations that the world thrusts upon each of us."

As a child, Ms. Fox lived in Zimbabwe where her parents worked as missionaries for Hope Fountain. There she was exposed firsthand to the kind of oppression she writes against. As a young adult, she attended drama school in England where she met her future husband. She married Malcolm Fox in 1969, and has one daughter, Chloe, now a journalist and high school teacher. Ms. Fox served as Assistant Professor at Flinders University in Adelaide, Australia for 24 years, a position from which she has since retired. Currently, she maintains a full schedule writing and traveling abroad both to promote her books and to champion literacy.

NOTES:

_____

_____

_____

_____

_____

_____

_____

_____

STORY CHARTS

The following pages contain story charts of the type presented in the live seminar *Teaching the Classics*. As is made clear in that seminar, a separate story chart may be constructed for each of the conflicts present in a work of fiction. In particular, the reader's decision as to the **climax** and central **themes** of the plot structure will depend upon his understanding of the story's central **conflict**. As a result, though the details of setting, characters, exposition, and conclusion may be identical from analysis to analysis, significant variation may be found in those components which appear down the center of the story chart: Conflict, Climax, and Theme. This of course results from the fact that literary interpretation is the work of active minds, and differences of opinion are to be expected – even encouraged!

For the teacher's information, one story chart has been filled in on the next page. In addition, a blank chart is included to allow the teacher to examine different conflicts in the same format.

Wilfrid Gordon McDonald Partridge by Mem Fox: Story Chart

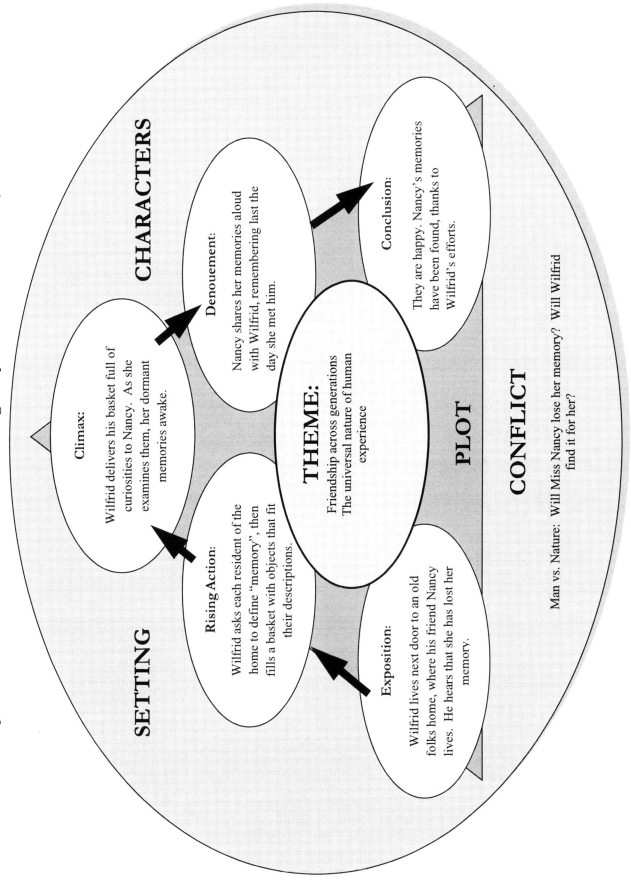

CHARACTERS

SETTING

Climax:
Wilfrid delivers his basket full of curiosities to Nancy. As she examines them, her dormant memories awake.

Denouement:
Nancy shares her memories aloud with Wilfrid, remembering last the day she met him.

Rising Action:
Wilfrid asks each resident of the home to define "memory", then fills a basket with objects that fit their descriptions.

THEME:
Friendship across generations
The universal nature of human experience

Conclusion:
They are happy. Nancy's memories have been found, thanks to Wilfrid's efforts.

Exposition:
Wilfrid lives next door to an old folks home, where his friend Nancy lives. He hears that she has lost her memory.

PLOT

CONFLICT

Man vs. Nature: Will Miss Nancy lose her memory? Will Wilfrid find it for her?

Wilfrid Gordon McDonald Partridge by Mem Fox: Blank Story Chart

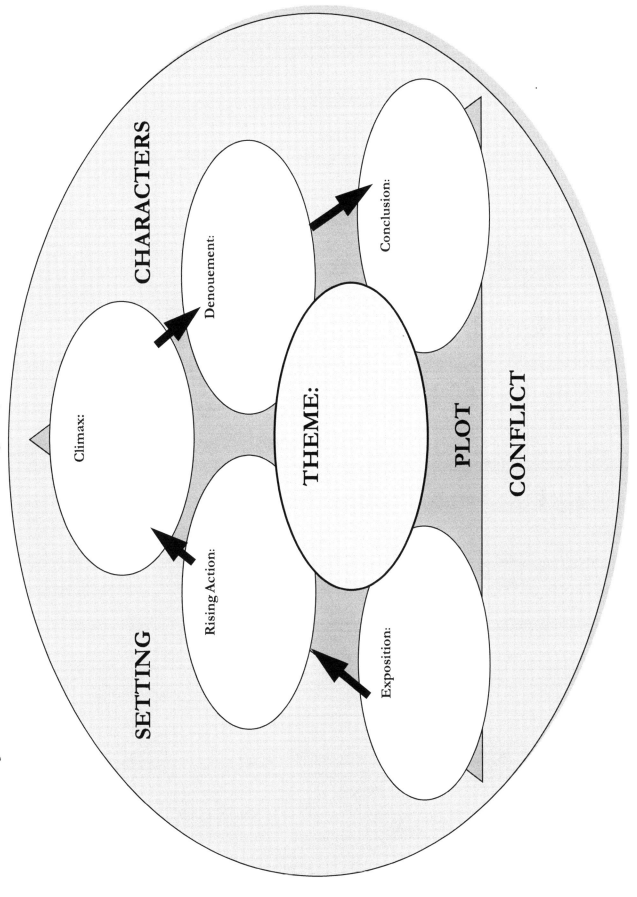

Jane Yolen's
Letting Swift River Go

Questions for Socratic Discussion
by Missy Andrews

CENTER FOR LIT

TABLE OF CONTENTS:
LETTING SWIFT RIVER GO

QUICK CARD

Reference	*Letting Swift River Go* by Jane Yolen ISBN-10: 0316968609 ISBN-13: 978-0316968607
Plot	When Sally Jane's hometown is evacuated to make room for the Quabbin reservoir, Sally struggles with feelings of displacement and loss.
Setting	• Swift River Valley, Massachusetts • 1920s • A small town • Sally's childhood
Characters	• Sally Jane (protagonist) • Sally's parents • Sally's friends: George Warren and Nancy Vaughan • Boston councilmen • Neighbors
Conflict	The Quabbin Reservoir Project swallows up the town of Swift River Valley and with it, Sally's childhood. (Man vs. Society, Man vs. Nature, Man vs. Self)
Theme	The passage of time; the transitory nature of life. The peace that comes with accepting things the way they are.
Literary Devices	Alliteration Assonance Sensory language Personification Simile Metaphor Imagery and Symbolism

QUESTIONS ABOUT STRUCTURE: SETTING

In what country or region does the story happen? (1a)

The story takes place in the Swift River Valley near the large city of Boston, Massachusetts.

What is the mood or atmosphere of the place where the story happens? Is it cheerful and sunny, or dark and bleak? What words, phrases or descriptions does the author use to create this atmosphere? (1d)

The mood of the place is sunny and peaceful. It is small town America, full of color and family history, a place with deep roots.

Among what kinds of people is the story set? What is their economic class? How do they live? Are they hopeful? Downtrodden? Depressed? Why? (1h)

The people of Swift River Valley are industrious and happy, involved in their community and linked to their forebears by the land.

Is the setting of the story important because of historical events which may have taken place there? How does this link help you understand the themes of the story? (1j)

The setting is important because of the historic inundation that was engineered there. Yet it is not singularly important since other inundations in other areas produced similar stories. This is a tribute to all such lost places.

When does this story happen? (2) How long a period of time does the story cover? A few minutes? A single day? A whole lifetime? (2b)

The story remembers a seven-year project to flood the Swift River Valley towns and is recollected by main character Sally Jane in retrospect.

In what time of life for the main characters do the events occur? Are they children? Are they just passing into adulthood? Are they already grownups? (2e)

The events remembered occur when the main character is only six. She remembers them as an adult.

In what intellectual period is the story set? What ideas were prevalent during the period of the story? Does the author deal with these ideas through his characters? Do the characters respond to social rules and customs that are the result of these ideas? (2f)

The author's note dates the event between 1927 and 1946. These years take in three US Presidencies including that of Calvin Coolidge ('23-'29), Herbert Hoover ('29-'33), and Franklin Roosevelt ('33-'45). The industrialization movement of the late 1800s and early 1900s caused a vast population surge in American cities. Urbanization found cities ill-designed to house such large numbers of residents. Overcrowding placed a strain on water supply and city sanitation; disease inevitably resulted.

The need for the Quabbin Reservoir was a local expression of this national problem. The project was precipitated by typhoid epidemics in Boston caused by contaminated water. In addition, a series of Boston fires ravaged the city because of the scarce water supply. City planners sought to solve these problems with the formation of this reservoir, the largest artificial domestic water supply system in the world at the time. This reservoir covers 56,000 acres and can contain 412 billion gallons of water.

NOTES:

_____

_____

_____

_____

_____

_____

_____

_____

_____

_____

QUESTIONS ABOUT STRUCTURE: CHARACTERS

Who is the story about? (3)

> The story is about residents of the Swift River Valley who in the 1920s were forced to deconstruct their homes and lives and move to accommodate the Quabbin Reservoir Project. In particular, the story's protagonist is six-year-old Swift River Valley resident, Sally Jane.

Is the character kind, gentle, stern, emotional, harsh, logical, rational, and compassionate or exacting…? Make up a list of adjectives that describe the protagonist. What words or actions on the protagonist's part make you choose the adjectives you do? (3f)

> Young Sally Jane is full of the wonder of childhood. She enjoys the abundant natural beauty of the valley, delighting in its familiar comfort and safety. She fishes with her friend and plays through the hot summer days. She traps fireflies in mason jars on summer nights, sleeping out under the spreading maples. She savors the sweet maple sap her father collects in the winter, and the feel of warm eiderdown against the chill. Moreover, she is disillusioned when the Boston City Council votes to take all these things from her forever.

Is the character a member of any particular religious or social group? If so, what do you know about this group? What motivates this group? What do its members feel to be important? (3l)

> Sally Jane is a resident of the Swift River Valley and one of the people relocated to accommodate the Boston city-dwellers who needed clean water. Sally Jane, 6-years-old, was among those people least considered in the move: the children.

What does the protagonist think is the most important thing in life? How do you know this? Does the protagonist say this out loud, or do his thoughts and actions give him away? (3m)

> As a child, Sally Jane considers her surroundings the most important thing in her life. As an adult, she struggles to let go of things wrested from her unwillingly in her youth.

How does the character of the protagonist reflect the values of the society (or individual) that produced the story? (3o)

> Sally's personality and values reflect those of many small town, country children. The places in their hometown have strong association with the people and events that mark their childhood. These landmarks are lost when the inundation covers them permanently.

Is the protagonist a sympathetic character? Do you identify with him and hope he will succeed? Do you pity him? Do you scorn or despise his weakness in some way? Why? (3q)

Sally's plight is sympathetic. Although perhaps only a handful of people can relate to the specific context of the story, most can relate to geographical changes that touch the historical landmarks of their childhood. Time marches ahead, sparing none.

Who else is the story about? (4)

Other protagonists include Sally Jane's friends and other residents of the Swift River Valley.

Is there a single character (or a group of characters) that opposes the protagonist in the story? (4a) Why does he oppose the protagonist? Does he merely belong to a different social group? Does he see the world in slightly different ways? Or is he an evil villain, like Shakespeare's Iago? (4f)

The antagonists are faceless – the Boston City Planners, the governor, progress. Of course, none of these mean harm to Sally Jane or her friends. Their exchange is purely business.

NOTES:

_____

_____

_____

_____

_____

_____

_____

_____

_____

_____

_____

QUESTIONS ABOUT STRUCTURE: CONFLICT AND PLOT

Fill in the blank: This story is about the protagonist trying to _____. (5a)

Sally Jane, grown to adulthood, contemplates the events of her childhood. She wants to recapture the past that has been lost.

Does the protagonist try to capture something? (5d)

More broadly, however, Sally Jane seeks peace with her past. This is an inner conflict.

Why can't she have it? (6) What kind of conflict is represented in this story? (6g-k)

On the surface, Sally's conflict is with the Boston City planners. (Man v. Man, Man v. Society) More broadly, Sally's struggle is against the inevitable encroachment of time (Man v. Nature), and with her own bitter loss (Man v. Self).

What happens in the story? (8) What major events take place in the story as a result of the conflict? (8a)

As a result of the vote to create the reservoir, the valley residents are forced to deconstruct their towns, move their dead, and evacuate the valley. Homes are abandoned or relocated. Graveyards are exhumed and relocated. Forests are felled. The towns are stripped of their life and beauty. Families move to new towns, some never to be seen again by Sally Jane. Friendships are lost. Finally, the waters cover the valley. The project takes seven years.

Does the protagonist get what he's after? (9a)

Time heals all wounds. A grown Sally Jane revisits the scene of the disaster with her father, skimming the surface of the Quabbin Reservoir by boat one evening. She peers through the water, vainly trying to revisit the dear places of her childhood. Yet they are covered over, never to be seen again.

What events form the highest point or climax of the story's tension? Are they circumstantial events, or emotional ones? Is the climax a spiritual or physical one? (9d)

This boat excursion represents the climax of the story. It's a spiritual climax for Sally.

Does the protagonist solve his own dilemma? Is it solved by some external source or third party? Is he helpless in the end to achieve his goal (like Frodo in Lord of the Rings), or does he triumph by virtue of his own efforts (Odysseus in <u>The Odyssey</u>)? (9e)

As Sally scoops the water of the reservoir into her hands to capture the starry sky that sparkles on its surface, she remembers her mother's childhood admonition to release the glowing fireflies she held captive in a jar. This metaphor links her to the past and enables her to release her sparkling, cherished memories to the deep of time. She can hold her childhood no more than she can hold the water or the starlight. It is a part of time – transient and ephemeral.

How does the story end? (10) Were you satisfied with the resolution? If not, why not? (10b)

The story's resolution is not completely satisfying, but it resonates with reality. Nothing could restore what Sally Jane lost. However, she can enjoy the memories by letting them go, and with them her bitterness. She must resolve to move forward and make new memories. She must live in the present.

NOTES:

_____

_____

_____

_____

_____

_____

_____

_____

_____

_____

QUESTIONS ABOUT STRUCTURE: THEME

What does the protagonist learn? (11) Is she ennobled in some way? (11c)

Sally Jane, affected by things common to man, is ennobled by her graceful response to them. Her strength is in her acquiescence to things she cannot change, her acceptance of the limitations of her "creaturehood."

What is the main idea of the story? (13)

The past cannot be contained or preserved. It is ephemeral like the blinking fireflies of Sally Jane's memory or the twinkling night sky. Peace comes from embracing the limitations of creaturehood rather than resisting them.

What answer does the story seem to suggest for the question, "What is a good life?" (13d)

The story suggests a good life is a life rooted in family and community.

What aspect of the human condition is brought to light and wondered at in this story? (13e)

The author contemplates the resilience of the human spirit.

NOTES:

_____

_____

_____

_____

_____

_____

_____

_____

QUESTIONS ABOUT STYLE

Does the author use the sounds of our language to create interest in his story? (14)

Alliteration and Assonance (14c, e)

"wind whispered…through…the willow by my…window"

"Georgie and I fished the Swift River in the bright days of summer; catching brown trout out of the pools with a pinhook…We played mumblety-peg… and picnicked…"

""We'd listen to the trains starting and stopping along Rabbit Run, their long whistles lowing into the dark, startling the screech owl off its perch on the great elm."

Sensory language

Gravestone stayed warm

We'd listen to the trains

See the fireflies

Taste the thin sweetness of maple sap

Does the author use descriptions and comparisons to create pictures in the reader's mind? (16)

Personification (16e-g)

Wind whispered

Similes (16d)

Papa had "bites under his eyes, swollen like tears."

Trees are "stacked like drinking straws"

"windows…stared out like empty eyes…"

Waters "rose like unfriendly neighbors"

Stars "winking on an off and on like fireflies"

Metaphors (16h-l)

Loggers (the governor's men) are "woodpeckers" to clear the scrub and brush, to cut down all the trees…"

Imagery (16a-c)

"I leaned over the side of the boat and caught the starry water in my cupped hands."

"I heard my mother's voice coming to me over the drowned years."

Does the author use the characters and events in his story to communicate a theme that goes beyond them in some way? (17)

Symbolism (17h, i)

The author uses fireflies' light to discuss elusive and transitory beauty. She suggests through extended metaphor that we do violence to such things by trying to possess them.

NOTES:

_____

_____

_____

_____

_____

_____

_____

_____

_____

_____

_____

QUESTIONS ABOUT CONTEXT

Who is the author? (18)

Born in New York, February 11, 1939, Jane Yolen became one of the most highly regarded children's authors of the twentieth century. After receiving a BA from Smith College in 1960, followed by a MA of Education in 1976 from the University of Massachusetts, Miss Yolen married David W. Stemple, a university professor. They parented two boys and a girl. Now the grandmother of 6, Ms. Yolen lives in Hatfield, Massachusetts where she continues her career as a writer and editor of children's books.

Hailed as America's Hans Christian Anderson, Miss Yolen has published 170 books. Among these are *The Emperor and the Kite*, *Owl Moon*, *All Those Secrets of the World*, and *Letting Swift River Go*. Writing stories she calls "rooted in family and self," Yolen's narratives follow in folklore tradition, the "universal human language." She is the winner of many awards including the society of Children's Writers Golden Kite Award, the World Fantasy Award, the Christopher Medal, the Kerlan Award, and the Caldecott Medal.

She lives near the Quabbin Reservoir in Hatfield, Massachusetts. She is of Jewish ancestry, and has belonged to the Quaker Friends church.

NOTES:

_____

_____

_____

_____

_____

_____

_____

_____

STORY CHARTS

The following pages contain story charts of the type presented in the live seminar *Teaching the Classics.* As is made clear in that seminar, a separate story chart may be constructed for each of the conflicts present in a work of fiction. In particular, the reader's decision as to the **climax** and central **themes** of the plot structure will depend upon his understanding of the story's central **conflict**. As a result, though the details of setting, characters, exposition, and conclusion may be identical from analysis to analysis, significant variation may be found in those components which appear down the center of the story chart: Conflict, Climax, and Theme. This of course results from the fact that literary interpretation is the work of active minds, and differences of opinion are to be expected – even encouraged!

For the teacher's information, one story chart has been filled in on the next page. In addition, a blank chart is included to allow the teacher to examine different conflicts in the same format.

Letting Swift River Go by Jane Yolen: Story Chart

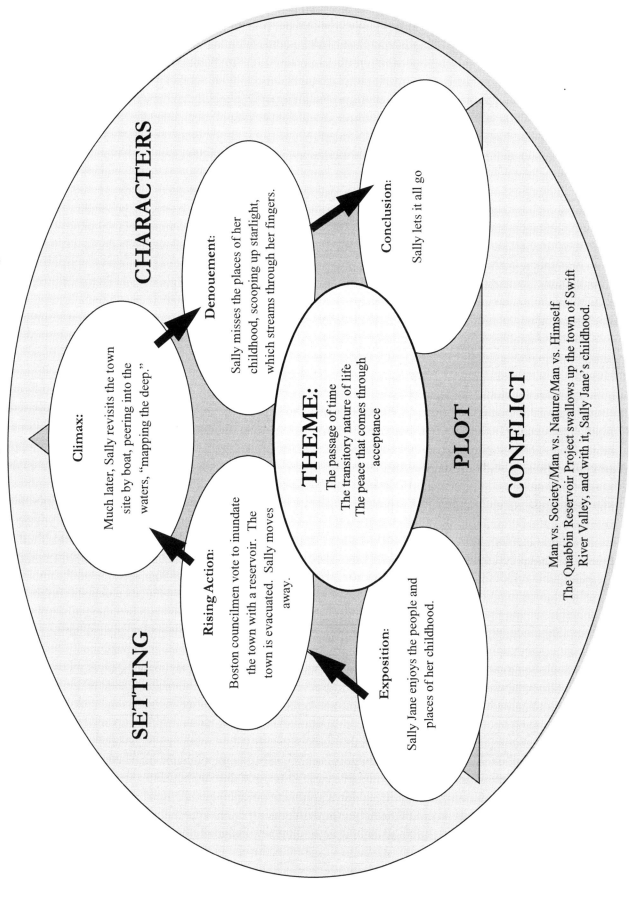

CHARACTERS

SETTING

Climax:
Much later, Sally revisits the town site by boat, peering into the waters, "mapping the deep."

Denouement:
Sally misses the places of her childhood, scooping up starlight, which streams through her fingers.

Conclusion:
Sally lets it all go

Rising Action:
Boston councilmen vote to inundate the town with a reservoir. The town is evacuated. Sally moves away.

THEME:
The passage of time
The transitory nature of life
The peace that comes through acceptance

Exposition:
Sally Jane enjoys the people and places of her childhood.

PLOT

CONFLICT

Man vs. Society/Man vs. Nature/Man vs. Himself
The Quabbin Reservoir Project swallows up the town of Swift River Valley, and with it, Sally Jane's childhood.

Letting Swift River Go by Jane Yolen: Blank Story Chart

CHARACTERS

SETTING

CONFLICT

PLOT

THEME:

Climax:

Denouement:

Conclusion:

Rising Action:

Exposition:

Patricia MacLachlan's
All the Places to Love

Questions for Socratic Discussion
by Missy Andrews

CENTER FOR LIT

TABLE OF CONTENTS:
ALL THE PLACES TO LOVE

QUICK CARD

Reference	*All the Places to Love* by Patricia MacLachlan ISBN-10: 0060210982 ISBN-13: 978-0060210984
Plot	The author traces the life of a boy who learns to love his home in the country by visiting the favorite places of his family members.
Setting	This book is all setting. It is fields, streams, hills, and valleys. It is sunlight and dappled forests, meadows and barns. It is a family homestead.
Characters	Eli, Mama, Papa, Grandfather, Grandmother, and Sylvie
Conflict	There is no obvious conflict. This is a contemplative, meditative slice of life. And yet, the theme of mortality runs throughout the story, creating a Man vs. Himself or Man vs. Nature conflict in the background.
Theme	An "homage to the American farm, re-creating all the glory and sweet simplicity of one family's connection to the land." (publisher) Eli learns that, no matter where his life may take him, he need look no farther than his home for all the places to love, and all the things that most matter. "Where else does an old turtle crossing the path make all the difference in the world?" The story praises the value and beauty of life's simplicity.
Literary Devices	This story reads like poetry. It is full of imagery. Take time to look for similes: comparisons using the words "like" or "as."

QUESTIONS FOR STRUCTURE: SETTING

Where does the story happen? (1)

The story is set in the countryside and encompasses a valley, a river, a hillside blueberry barren, a meadow, and the narrator's family farm, which nestles among these. Here, the narrator asserts, are "all the places to love." Because each place is a special haunt of one of the narrator's family members, each becomes by extension an important place to him as well.

The meadows and hay fields, which become marshes in springtime, are favorite romping grounds for the dogs. The farm's fields of rich, sweet dirt are his papa's realm. His grandmother shares with him her love of the river. His mother prefers the open skies of the blueberry barren. Eli's grandfather loves his silent barn best of all places. There he carves the names of his family members in the bulky rafters as permanent memorials.

Not only is the story's setting rich, but it also carries the conflict, becoming the vehicle for thematic content. These lovely and dear places represent more than mere scenic beauty. Associated with the persons who love them, they remain permanent landmarks of people who may not remain in those places forever. Not only may circumstances require that they move to other locales, but their humanity implies mortality; theirs are lives that will pass. These places, imbued by association with the personality of their lovers, will survive the passage of time. For this reason, they represent a permanent bridge or continuum between generations, concrete symbols that carry the resolution and theme of the story.

At what stage in the lives of the main characters do the events take place? (2e)

The story happens in the narrator's childhood. A young boy, he is learning from his family what is important in life. Not only is he learning how to be a man, but also how to be a contributing member of his family group. What does the group value? What makes them all tick? How can he absorb the best of each of his family members and make it a part of himself? Who will he be? Eli's growing identity is wrapped up in the people and places of the story.

NOTES:

_____

_____

_____

_____

_____

_____

_____

_____

_____

_____

_____

_____

_____

_____

_____

_____

QUESTIONS ABOUT STRUCTURE: CHARACTERS

Who is the story about? (3)

Eli is the young narrator and protagonist of the story. His first person remarks explain the significance of place, the land, to his readers. Since he is no more than eight or nine years old, these places and people constitute his entire world.

Who else is the story about? (4)

The other family members, all adults, feel the story's unspoken conflict in a way Eli hasn't yet. Eli is a child and hasn't lost any of the people who make the places special. The older characters are better acquainted with the temporal nature of life. They feel the conflict, the significance of life, more keenly. For example, Grandfather cries when Eli's sister, Sylvie, is born.

Mama- She carries Eli on romps through fields, sharing her family places with him. Her spot is the open blueberry barren where she can see both the sun's rising and setting.

Grandmother – Present at both Eli and Sylvie's births, she baptizes them with the valley breeze and initiates them in the ways of the glistening, gurgling river.

Grandfather – His love for family members is inscribed on the rafters of his favorite place, the silent, languid barn.

Father – One with the fields he works, he savors their "sweet dirt," carrying it home in his pockets.

Sylvie – When Eli's baby sister is born, Eli comes into his own. Now it's his turn to share the places to love. It is his turn participate in the transfer of family values to another generation.

NOTES:

_____

_____

_____

_____

QUESTIONS ABOUT STRUCTURE: CONFLICT AND PLOT

As mentioned in notes about setting, this haunting piece reads more like a series of still life pictures or a poem than a story. The setting is inherently peaceful. Nothing disturbs the tranquil scene. Life's simplest experiences are related: picking blueberries, walking in the fields, sailing bark boats down river, watching turtles, and listening to cows chew their cud through the lazy afternoon hours. Is there any conflict within the pages of this narrative?

All students of literature learn early that without conflict, there can be no story. Place and characters fail to live, move, and breathe without the motivation of conflict animating them.

While the conflict within this narrative is as quiet as the scenes described, it does exist. Driving the story forward and imbuing the places with significance is the underlying tension created by the inevitable passage of time. Parents are aging. Children are growing. All that is dear is being transferred from parent, to child, to child. The land is the wineskin that holds the wine of these lives together. It is the glue that binds each generation to the next. It will remain after these lives have passed and will continue to symbolize the ideas and values of the people with whom it was associated.

To arrive at a discussion of these themes with students, contemplate the following questions:

What does the protagonist want? (5)

> Eli wants to enjoy the places he's been taught and given to love, and to share them with his baby sister, teaching her to love them as well. He wants to own his family membership and to preserve his family heritage.

Why can't he have it? Does his age, economic class, race, or sex stand in his way? (6d) Is he racing against time? (6e)

> Eli is indeed racing against time, because time brings changes. Eli must remember, cherish, and share these places in order to preserve them. He must remember the places and the people associated with them regardless of where he may go. He must internalize the value of these places, and make them his own. He must choose to value his heritage and transfer it.

What sort of conflict is represented in this story? (6h)

> Since time is a sort of silent antagonist in this story, reminding us of the impermanence of earthly life, this is a Man vs. Nature conflict. Time is meanly impersonal. Established as a part of God's created order, it "obeys no man," but only God, reminding us by its constant passage that we are but creatures.

What other problems are there in the story? What other conflicts and themes does the story articulate? (7)

In addition to the underlying threat of change and mortality, the story follows Eli's growth to early maturity. That is, Eli wants to discover his own "place." This place is both literal, a special haunt of his very own, and symbolic, a place only he can fill in the family order. This is a coming of age story. Eli becomes one of the givers in the story – one of the ones who know all the places to love.

Remember that a story's themes are directly related to its conflicts. Since the conflicts in this story are subtle, a discussion of them will develop students' understanding of conflict. Not all antagonists are human; not all are wicked. Yet they remain conflicts as they work against the protagonist's desires.

In this story, Eli probably isn't aware of just why the land is valuable. He isn't yet aware of his or his loved ones' mortality, nor is he as moved by the preciousness of life as his grandfather is. He just knows he wants to keep his childhood "snapshots" forever. They capture time. They substantiate and validate a changing reality. They embody all that has made him who he is, the admixture of the family and experiences that have shaped him. These places are to cherish and to share with his family. He'll start with his baby sister. "Sylvie," he'll say, "here's my favorite place. Let's find yours. This is how to live well. Listen. Look. Value. Remember. Share…" And he'll be right, of course.

What happens in the story? (8)

Eli visits all the special places his family loves. As he does so, he not only grows to appreciate the magical qualities of each locale, but also develops special relationships with the members who share them with him.

–Eli is born. His grandmother wraps him in a blanket made of wool from the sheep she raised. She raises him to the window to show him the family land.

–Grandfather carves Eli's name into his favorite place, the barn, making him a part of the family and its heritage.

–Mama shares the meadow.

–Father shares his wisdom and the sweet soil of his fields.

–Grandmother shares the river.

–Eli discovers the marsh.

–Mother shares the blueberry barren.

–Grandfather shares the barn where soon, he and Eli together await the arrival of a new family member.

How is the main problem solved? (9) Does the protagonist get what he's after? (9a)

When Sylvie is born, Eli participates in the process of bringing another member into his family circle. He has come of age. Now it is his privilege to share with another the things that were given to him. He has been shown the places to love, and he has grown to love them himself. He has given himself to the family vision, and will share in their purpose – enjoying one another and creaturehood. "Someday I might live in the city. Someday I might live by the sea. But soon I will carry Sylvie on my shoulders through the fields; I will send her messages downriver in small boats; and I will watch her at the top of the hill, trying to touch the sky. I will show her my favorite place, the marsh, where ducklings follow their mother like tiny tumbles of leaves." Eli has discovered his own place, both physically and metaphorically speaking.

Is the situation pleasantly resolved, or is it resolved in a terrible way? (9c)

In a greater sense, the underlying conflict of mortality is softened by this transferred vision. The awfulness of mortality is swallowed up in something larger than the individual, yet simultaneously a part of the individual: the family. The transfer of values and vision from generation to generation causes a man to live beyond his grave in the lives of his descendants. While man cannot live forever, he can become a part of something that extends beyond his lifetime and so influence those he may never meet.

NOTES:

_____

_____

_____

_____

_____

_____

_____

_____

_____

QUESTIONS ABOUT STRUCTURE: THEME

What does the protagonist learn? (11) Is he changed in his mind or heart by the events of the story? (11a)

Eli learns that "all the places to love" are among his people. He is inducted into membership in his family circle.

Does he begin to act differently? In what way? (11b)

Eli's actions demonstrate that he has internalized all that his family has given him. He has become a part of something larger than himself and recognizes that, regardless of what he will do individually throughout the course of his life, something larger than himself exists there on the family land – something to which he belongs - something good and worthy.

Does the main character explain to the reader his perspective on the events that have transpired? (11e)

Eli vows to share what he's learned with his sister. "All the places to love are here, I'll tell her, no matter where you may live. Where else, I will say, does an old turtle crossing the path make all the difference in the world?"

Does the story deal with universal themes? (13a)

The story deals with universal themes like mortality, the fleeting passage of time, and coming of age. It speaks of family heritage and values, the significance of the land, and generational continuity.

Does the story offer an answer to a particular problem associated with one of those themes? (13b)

The author suggests that family offers the individual a way to transcend mortality by influencing the next generation. Family is the place where one can leave a permanent mark on the world. In like manner, the land is significant in the story. Outlasting the characters of the story, unmarked by mortality, it serves as a touchstone between the generations, a staying influence, an opportunity and invitation to build something larger than the individual.

What answer does the story seem to suggest for the question, "What is a good life?" (13d)

The story suggests that a good life is a life lived in relationship with others. A good life is a life that embraces creaturehood, enjoying its privileges and transcending its limitations. Not only is a good life gained by embracing the limitations of nature, but also by associating with nature. By connecting with nature – appreciating and living close to it – the individual etches himself into the permanence of place. He becomes attached to the land. Others know him by his land and remember him in connection with it. The land is a part of him. It will receive him, and he will leave it to his progeny. This adds importance to the generational transfer of vision. Should one of the members fail to grasp the importance of place, all that they have built may be lost.

NOTES:

_____

_____

_____

_____

_____

_____

_____

_____

_____

_____

_____

QUESTIONS ABOUT STYLE

Does the author use the sounds of our language to create interest in the story? (14)

This story reads like poetry, and that's largely because of the proliferation of literary devices that embellish the text.

Sensory language makes the story live.

"What I heard first…" (hear)

"What I saw first…" (see)

"Raucous black grackles…" (hear)

"That sound like a whisper…" (hear)

"The bed was warm when I touched it."(feel)

"Where else can I see the sun rise…?" (see)

"Grandma sailed little bark boats downriver with messages…" (see)

"Where else does an old turtle crossing the road…" (see)

"My grandfather's barn is sweet-smelling and dark and cool." (smell, see, feels)

"Where else can the soft sound of cows chewing…" (hear)

Alliteration (14e)

"sly smiles" of the dogs

"Papa and I plowed"

"Where else is soil so sweet?"

"Papa put a handful of dirt in his pocket"

""meadow turned to marsh…"

"Cattails stood…and killdeers called"

"marsh marigolds"

"footprints for us to find"

Consonance (14d)

"Raucous bla<u>ck</u> gra<u>ck</u>les"

Does the author use descriptions and comparisons to create pictures in the reader's mind? (15)

Similes (15d)

"Crows in the dirt that swaggered like pirates"

"trout flashed like jewels"

"Cattails stood like guards…"

"Leather harnesses hang like paintings against old wood; and hay dust floats like gold in the air."

"Where ducklings follow their mother like tiny tumbles of leaves."

Repetition of Words

"Rock to rock to rock…"

"Someday I might…"

"Where else…?"

NOTES:

_____

_____

_____

_____

_____

_____

QUESTIONS ABOUT CONTEXT

Who is the author? (18)

Patricia MacLachlan began her writing career at 35-years-old. The mother of three, her interest in writing stems from her concern for families and children. A graduate of University of Connecticut, she has taught English, written journal articles, and served on a local family agency board researching and writing about adoption and foster mothers. Her interest in children's literature inevitably grew out of these experiences.

Although Ms. MacLachlan currently resides in Massachusetts, she confesses a strong connection to the Wyoming prairies of her childhood. As evidence of this heart connection, she reportedly carries with her a small bag of prairie dirt. This love of place is evident in her works, which are laced with scenes of prairie and sea.

When questioned concerning her writing methods, she states that character forms the backbone of her stories. Indeed, memorable characters have been born from her pen in acclaimed favorites *Sarah, Plain and Tall*, *Skylark*, *Baby*, *Journey*, *Arthur for the Very First Time*, *The Facts and Fictions of Minna Pratt*, and *Unclaimed Treasures*.

While she enjoys a busy career as a writer and speaker, Ms. MacLachlan finds time to teach a children's literature course at Smith College. She recently published a children's book with her daughter, Emily, entitled *Painting the Wind*. Her work has garnered recognition such as the Golden Kite Award and the Scott O'Dell Award for Historical Fiction for Children. Additionally, several of her books have enjoyed a place on the ALA's Notable Children's Books list.

NOTES:

_____

_____

_____

_____

_____

_____

_____

_____

STORY CHARTS

The following pages contain story charts of the type presented in the live seminar *Teaching the Classics.* As is made clear in that seminar, a separate story chart may be constructed for each of the conflicts present in a work of fiction. In particular, the reader's decision as to the **climax** and central **themes** of the plot structure will depend upon his understanding of the story's central **conflict**. As a result, though the details of setting, characters, exposition, and conclusion may be identical from analysis to analysis, significant variation may be found in those components which appear down the center of the story chart: Conflict, Climax, and Theme. This of course results from the fact that literary interpretation is the work of active minds, and differences of opinion are to be expected – even encouraged!

For the teacher's information, one story chart has been filled in on the next page. In addition, a blank chart is included to allow the teacher to examine different conflicts in the same format.

All the Places to Love by Patricia MacLachlan: Story Chart

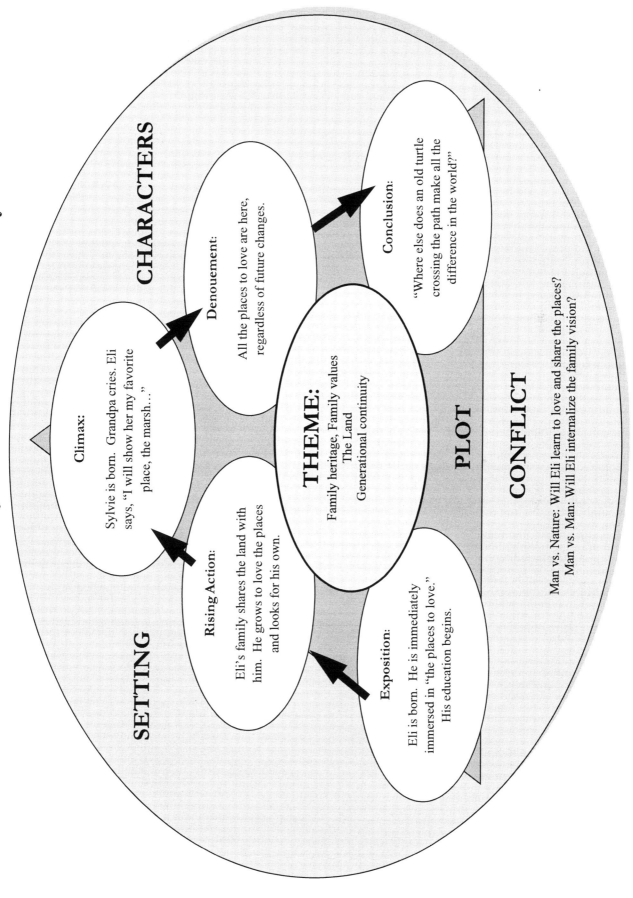

CHARACTERS

SETTING

THEME:
Family heritage, Family values
The Land
Generational continuity

PLOT

CONFLICT

Climax:
Sylvie is born. Grandpa cries. Eli says, "I will show her my favorite place, the marsh…"

Denouement:
All the places to love are here, regardless of future changes.

Conclusion:
"Where else does an old turtle crossing the path make all the difference in the world?"

Rising Action:
Eli's family shares the land with him. He grows to love the places and looks for his own.

Exposition:
Eli is born. He is immediately immersed in "the places to love." His education begins.

Man *vs.* Nature: Will Eli learn to love and share the places?
Man *vs.* Man: Will Eli internalize the family vision?

All the Places to Love by Patricia MacLachlan: Blank Story Chart

CHARACTERS

SETTING

CONFLICT

PLOT

THEME:

Climax:

Denouement:

Rising Action:

Exposition:

Conclusion:

Master the Method

TEACHING THE
CLASSICS

Second Edition
by Adam and Missy Andrews

Now with 2 hours and 25 pages of additional content, it's
the same DVD seminar for the method you love with a
beautiful new look and even more training to equip you to
have meaningful discussions about any work of literature.

www.centerforlit.com/teaching-the-classics

Did you enjoy this Ready Readers?
Check out the rest in the series!

Children's Literature

Elementary Literature

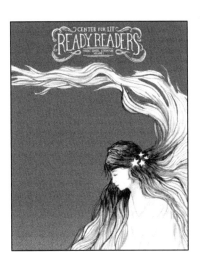

Middle School Literature

High School Literature

...The Chronicles of Narnia and more!